ADVANTAGE Test Prep

Grade 8

Table of Contents

Introduction 3

Introduction to Reading 6
Nonfiction Reading Selection:
  An Early River Civilization .. 7
Vocabulary
Words in Context............... 8
Interpret Figurative Language 9
Comprehension
Summarize 10
Classify Information 11
Compare and Contrast 12
Fiction Reading Selection:
  The Rich Merchant 13
Vocabulary
Denotation and Connotation 14
Comprehension
Make Predictions 15
Relevant and Irrelevant
  Information 16
Nonfiction Reading Selection:
  Let's Get Busy! 17
Vocabulary
Transitional Words 18
Comprehension
Persuasive Techniques 19
Distinguish Fact and Opinion..... 20
Poetry Reading Selection:
  Two Poems by Li Bo 21
Comprehension
Setting........................ 22
Point of View 23

Graphic Information
Forms 24
Tables......................... 25
Charts......................... 26
Maps 27
References
Table of Contents.............. 28
Dictionary Entry 29

Introduction to Writing: Understanding
  Writing Prompts 30
Understanding Scoring Rubrics .. 31
Brainstorm and Organize
  Your Ideas................. 32
Writing Prompt 33
Plan and Write Your First Draft... 34
Edit Your First Draft............ 36
Write Your Final Draft 37
Give Yourself a Score 39

Introduction to Language 40
Mechanics
Punctuation and Capitalization... 41
Hyphens...................... 42
Parentheses and Brackets 43
Commas and Semicolons 44
Grammar and Usage
Infinitives and Participles....... 45
Gerunds and Gerund Phrases 46
Pronouns and Antecedents....... 47
Parts of Speech................ 48

Table of Contents

Sentence Structure
Types of Sentences............. 49
Lively Sentences 50
Parallel Construction 51
Coordination, Subordination
  and Apposition............. 52

Spelling
Inflected Endings 53
Frequently Misspelled Words..... 54

Introduction to Math 55

Number Sense and Numeration
Compare and Order Integers
  and Fractions................ 56
Convert Decimals to Scientific
  Notation.................... 57
Add and Subtract Numbers Written
  in Scientific Notation 58

Computation and Operations
Add and Subtract Fractions with
  Unlike Denominators 59
Multiply Integers 60
Divide Decimals 61

Estimation and Number Theory
Check the Reasonableness of
  an Answer................. 62
Least Common Denominator 63
Find Ratios 64

Measurement
Volume of a Solid 65
Solve Problems Involving
  Scale Factors................ 66
Solve Problems Involving Rates ... 67

Geometry
Pythagorean Relationship........ 68
Congruence and Similarity....... 69
Examine Shapes on a
  Coordinate Grid............ 70

Algebraic Thinking
Evaluate Expressions 71
Solve Equations with
  Two Variables 72
Graph Linear Equations 73

Data Analysis and Probability
Find Measures of Center
  and Spread 74
Compute Probabilities for
  Simple Compound Events.... 75
Represent Data Graphically 76

Problem Solving
Solve a Multi-Step Problem 77
Solve a Proportion Problem 78

Practice Test Introduction 79
Student Information Sheet 80
Practice Test Answer Sheet....... 81
Practice Test: Reading 82
Practice Test: Writing 90
Practice Test: Language 95
Practice Test: Mathematics 101

Answer Key 109

CREDITS

Concept Development: Kent Publishing Services, Inc.
Written by: Jeff Putnam
Design: Moonhee Pak
Production: Signature Design Group, Inc.
Art Director: Tom Cochrane
Project Director: Carolea Williams

© 2005 Creative Teaching Press, Inc., Huntington Beach, CA 92649
Reproduction of activities in any manner for use in the classroom and not for commercial sale is permissible.
Reproduction of these materials for an entire school or for a school system is strictly prohibited.

Introduction

Testing in reading, writing, language, and mathematics have taken on a large role in education today. This workbook is designed to help students practice the skills and strategies that they will encounter on standardized and proficiency tests. Even if students don't have to take these tests, they will benefit from practicing the skills and strategies taught in this workbook.

Standardized Tests

Standardized tests are administered in the exact same way to hundreds of thousands of students across the United States. They are also referred to as *norm-referenced tests*. Norms give educators a common standard of measurement of students' skills and abilities across the country. Students are ranked according to their test scores and then assigned a percentile ranking. For example, a percentile score of 85 means a student scored higher than 85 percent of the students who also took the same test.

Proficiency Tests

Many states develop their own statewide proficiency tests. Proficiency tests are also known as *criterion-referenced* tests. This means that the test is based on a list of standards and skills (also called criteria). States develop standards for what students should know at each grade level. The proficiency test evaluates a student's mastery of set standards.

Standardized tests and proficiency tests look similar. However, their measurement is different. A proficiency test measures a student's mastery of set standards. A standardized test compares a student's achievement to others who took the same test.

Although the measurement is different, standardized and proficiency tests do have similarities in that they are used to:
- evaluate students' progress, strengths, and weaknesses.
- select students for remedial or achievement programs.
- tell educators where and how school systems can be improved.
- evaluate the success of school programs.
- help educators develop programs to suit their students' specific needs.

Both of these types of achievement tests are administered essentially the same way. They ask multiple-choice and open-response questions, and they have time limits. An important goal of this workbook is to teach test-taking strategies so that no matter which test your child is required to take, he or she will be successful.

Introduction

Preparing for Tests

The more students are prepared for taking standardized and proficiency tests, the higher they will perform on those tests. A student who understands the skills commonly measured and who practices test-taking strategies is more likely to be a successful test-taker. The more the student knows what to expect, the more comfortable the student will be in the actual test-taking situations.

Many tests were reviewed in developing the material for this workbook. They include the following:
- **California Achievement Tests (CAT)**
- **Comprehensive Test of Basic Skills (CTBS)**
- **TerraNova**
- **Iowa Test of Basic Skills (ITBS)**
- **Metropolitan Achievement Tests (MAT)**
- **Stanford Achievement Tests (SAT)**
- **Texas Assessment of Knowledge and Skills (TAKS)**

It is important to remember that standardized and proficiency tests are only one measure of student achievement. Teachers use many other methods to gain insights into each student's skills, abilities, and knowledge. It is a good idea to speak with your child's teacher to discuss and understand all the methods used in evaluating your child.

Introduction

How Can Parents Help Students Take Standardized Tests Successfully?

The following list includes suggestions on how to help prepare students to do their best on standardized tests.

Tips for Parents
- Monitor your child's progress.
- Get to know your child's teacher; find out what he or she thinks you can do to best help your child at home.
- Be informed about your state's testing requirements.
- Motivate your child to prepare.
- Help your child structure a quiet place and time away from distractions to do homework.
- Find learning experiences in everyday life such as making change, reading signs, preparing food, or walking outside.
- Make sure your child is getting the sleep and nutrition he or she needs to succeed.
- Always nurture your child's curiosity and desire to learn.
- Encourage your child to learn about computers and technology.
- Encourage your child to take tests seriously, but to value learning and giving one's best efforts.
- Notice academic efforts your child is making and support and acknowledge what you see.

Where Can I Learn More About Testing?

National Center for Fair and Open Testing, Inc. (FairTest)
342 Broadway
Cambridge, MA 02139
http://www.fairtest.org/

Visit the Web site of the Department of Education for your state. Most states post information about standardized and proficiency tests that they administer to students.

Introduction to Reading

Reading is a skill that will help you do well in school as well as in life. The more you read, the *better* you will read—it's that simple. And the better you read, the more you'll enjoy it and the higher you'll score on standardized tests. Read as much as you can. Choose many different types of reading materials. Read by yourself or with others. Read aloud or silently. When you read stories, think about how they develop and progress.

Nearly every standardized or proficiency test includes a section on reading. The reading passages may be fiction, nonfiction, or poetry. They may also include graphic information, such as maps, graphs, charts, or time lines, or reference information such as indexes or dictionary entries. You will be asked to recall, interpret, and reflect on what you read.

The following pages give a review of reading skills. You will practice the skills with questions just like the ones on standardized tests. Practicing these skills now will help you perform better on test day. In this workbook section, you will learn to:

- use **context** clues to find the meaning of words or examine **roots**, **prefixes**, and **suffixes**.
- interpret **figurative language**.
- **summarize** texts.
- **classify** information.
- **compare** and **contrast** information.
- examine **denotative** and **connotative meanings**.
- make **predictions**.
- distinguish between **relevant** and **irrelevant information**.
- identify **transitional words**.
- identify **persuasive techniques**.
- distinguish between **fact** and **opinion**.
- analyze literary devices such as **setting** and **point of view**.
- read and understand **forms**, **tables**, **charts**, and **maps**.
- use a **table of contents**.
- read a **dictionary entry**.

Read the selection, *An Early River Civilization*. Then complete the activities on pages 8 through 12.

An Early River Civilization

The world's first civilizations grew up in river valleys. River valleys were attractive to early peoples for several reasons. Perhaps most importantly, the water from the rivers could be used to irrigate crop fields, as well as provide water for drinking and other purposes. The fish and other animals found in rivers offered a ready source of food. Rivers also attracted wildlife such as birds and animals, which were also good sources of food.

Yet another advantage of settling near rivers was the ease of transportation. Traveling over land could be slow and dangerous. Water transportation, however, could be fast and relatively easy. When danger threatened, rivers offered a means of escape.

Many great early civilizations are associated with rivers. Think of Egypt and the Nile, Mesopotamia and the Tigris and Euphrates, and India and the Indus and Ganges. In ancient China, the river that saw the dawn of its civilization was the mighty Huang He, or Yellow River. Along its banks, in the northern part of the country, the first of China's many dynasties, or groups of related rulers, took root.

China's first dynasty is known as the Shang. The Shang rulers lived from about 1750 to 1122 B.C. Their capital was a city in the Huang He valley called Anyan. Shang society was basically agricultural and depended on the bounty of the great river. As it flowed toward the Yellow Sea in the East, it deposited a rich yellow soil along its valley. This soil, called *loess*, helped the land remain fertile. The Huang He was not always a good neighbor, however. Sometimes, heavy rains caused it to overflow its banks. The result was terrible floods that took a dreadful toll on the Shang people.

In addition to farming, the Shang people also became very skilled in casting bronze weapons, pots, masks, and other objects. Smaller bronze objects were often used in religious services and rituals to honor ancestors. Bronze objects were frequently buried with important people, perhaps to help them in the next life. Today, collectors eagerly seek Shang bronzes.

Much of what we know about these ancient people comes from an unusual source. The Shang believed they could communicate with supernatural beings. In particular, the Shang people thought that these gods could give them advice on worldly affairs such as how to run the government, whether to go to war, or how to cure the ruler's illness. To get their questions to the gods, Shang priests invented the first Chinese writing. The priests then scratched their questions onto animal bones. Heated metal rods were stuck into the bones, known as oracle bones, causing a series of cracks. The priests studied the patterns of cracks, interpreting them as answers from the gods. The bones were carefully stored. Many have survived to our time to speak to us. Through them we have been able to learn about these ancient people and the society they created.

VOCABULARY

KNOW THE SKILL: WORDS IN CONTEXT

Some test questions ask you to figure out the meaning of a word. Often you can guess the meaning of the word by thinking about the word's context. **Context** is the meanings of the other words and phrases around an unknown word. Context determines or influences the meaning of words.

DURING THE TEST

To learn from the context what a word means, look for the verb or subject of the sentences around it. These words will give you clues about the unknown word.

TEST EXAMPLE

1. Read the following sentence from the selection.
   Heated metal rods were stuck into the bones, known as oracle bones, causing a series of cracks.
   Which answer is a synonym for *oracle*?
   - Ⓐ ancient
   - Ⓑ religious
   - Ⓒ supernatural
   - Ⓓ fortune-telling

THINK ABOUT THE ANSWER

The correct answer is option D, *fortune-telling*. The subject of the paragraph is how priests used the bones to look into the future. Option A, *ancient* is incorrect because the text tells us that the bones were from dead animals, not old sources. Options B and C make sense, because the bones were used in religious ceremonies to contact supernatural beings, but they do not mean the same thing as *fortune-telling* and *oracle*.

NOW YOU TRY IT

2. Read the following sentence from the selection.
   Shang society was basically agricultural and depended on the bounty of the great river.
   Choose the word that means the same thing as *bounty*.
   - Ⓕ gifts
   - Ⓖ water
   - Ⓗ fertility
   - Ⓙ agriculture

Check your answer on page 109.

Get Outta Here!
When answering context vocabulary questions like these, plug each choice into the sentence and ask yourself if it makes sense. Some will not, and you can eliminate these right away.

Vocabulary

KNOW THE SKILL: INTERPRET FIGURATIVE LANGUAGE

Figurative language is words used in a way different from their literal meaning to create variety or interest. Consider this sentence: *The shadows of the night crept up on the campsite.* In this example, the night's shadows do not literally take steps. The author is using the word *crept* figuratively to compare the night's shadows to an animal stalking, or creeping up on, the campers.

DURING THE TEST

Be on the lookout for words used in a way that departs from their literal, or exact, meaning. If asked to identify or explain figurative language, think about how the use of the nonliteral meaning adds interest and variety to the text.

TEST EXAMPLE

1. Which sentence from the selection uses figurative language?
   - Ⓐ The priests then scratched their questions onto animal bones.
   - Ⓑ The fish and other animals found in rivers offered a ready source of food.
   - Ⓒ Bronze objects were frequently buried with important people, perhaps to help them in the next life.
   - Ⓓ Along its banks, in the northern part of the country, the first of China's many dynasties, or groups of related rulers, took root.

THINK ABOUT THE ANSWER

Option D is correct. By using the word *root*, the writer compares the beginnings of Chinese civilization to a tree putting down roots.

NOW YOU TRY IT

2. Which sentence from the selection uses figurative language?
   - Ⓕ Many have survived to our time to speak to us.
   - Ⓖ Yet another advantage of settling near rivers was the ease of transportation.
   - Ⓗ Through them we have been able to learn about these ancient people and the society they created.
   - Ⓙ Smaller bronze objects were often used in religious services and rituals to honor ancestors.

Check your answer on page 109.

COMPREHENSION

KNOW THE SKILL: SUMMARIZE

Some test questions will ask you to summarize part or all of a selection. To summarize a text means to restate or paraphrase the important points using your own words.

DURING THE TEST

If you are asked to summarize a selection, you may find it helpful to make check marks near or underline the important points. That way, you can go back and easily see which information to include in the summary. A one-sentence summary might be very similar to a topic sentence of a paragraph.

TEST EXAMPLE

1 Write a one-sentence summary of the first paragraph of the selection.

_____
_____
_____

THINK ABOUT THE ANSWER

You could have written something like this: *For a variety of beneficial reasons, early peoples decided to build their civilizations near rivers.* The paragraph is a discussion of reasons why rivers offered early peoples a good place to settle.

NOW YOU TRY IT

2 Write a summary of the last paragraph of the selection.

_____
_____
_____

Check your answer on page 109.

Just the Main ideas
Keep this suggestion in mind when answering a question that asks you to summarize; your summary should contain few, if any details, and must include all the important main ideas.

COMPREHENSION

KNOW THE SKILL: CLASSIFY INFORMATION

Some test questions will ask you to classify different kinds of information in a text. To classify information means to divide it into different groups or categories based on how it is used in the text or what kind of details it provides. Being able to classify will help you divide large amounts of information into smaller, more manageable categories.

DURING THE TEST

Questions may ask you to name the general categories of a selection and then classify details into each. As you read, underline words and phrases that seem to belong to one or another major category of information. Then you'll be able to go back and skim for details to classify into the categories.

TEST EXAMPLE

1. What two elements of Shang culture are discussed in the selection?
   - Ⓐ river transportation and the use of oracle bones
   - Ⓑ agriculture and the importance of river wildlife
   - Ⓒ the use of oracle bones and the casting of bronze objects
   - Ⓓ the casting of bronze objects and flooding of the Huang He

THINK ABOUT THE ANSWER

Option C is correct. The selection's information about Shang culture can be classified into two categories: *oracle bones* and *bronze casting*. Much of the information in the text consists of details about these two main ideas.

NOW YOU TRY IT

2. What is the best category name for this information from the text?
   provided water, served as a source of food, easy transportation, and means of quick escape
   - Ⓕ why the Shang settled near the Huang He
   - Ⓖ why early people settled near rivers
   - Ⓗ Egypt, Mesopotamia, and India
   - Ⓙ the Shang civilization

Check your answer on page 109.

Like an Outline
It may be helpful to think about classifying as a kind of outline. The category name is a general, major head, while the details under it must be related and more specific.

COMPREHENSION

KNOW THE SKILL: COMPARE AND CONTRAST

Some test questions will ask you to compare and contrast different information. **Comparing** things means telling how they are similar. **Contrasting** means telling how they are different.

DURING THE TEST

A question might ask you how two ideas, people, objects, or other things are the same or how they are different. Word clues in the text that signal a comparison are *like*, *same as*, and *similar*. Those that signal a contrast are *on the other hand*, *however*, and *but*. Look for these words in the selection when you are asked to compare or contrast on a test question.

TEST EXAMPLE

1. Write two sentences to explain how Shang bronzes and oracle bones were similar.

   _____
   _____
   _____

THINK ABOUT THE ANSWER

A correct answer could have made these points: both were used for religious purposes; both tell us about how the Shang people lived.

NOW YOU TRY IT

2. Write two sentences to explain how Shang bronzes and oracle bones were different.

   _____
   _____
   _____

Check your answer on page 109.

Have a Positive Attitude
A positive attitude helps in all you do. Have self-confidence and think positive thoughts.

Read the story, The Rich Merchant, based on an old Chinese story. Then complete the activities on pages 14 through 16.

The Rich Merchant

There once was a rich merchant from the town of Shansi. He took a business trip to the capital city. He went there to try to get an official position by bribing some important people. To pay the bribe, he took with him a lot of money.

One day while the merchant was in the capital city, a very poor old man came to see him at his hotel. He asked to see the merchant, but the merchant ignored the poor old man. Finally, after waiting for days, the merchant agreed to see the old man. "I'm very poor," the old man said timidly.

"So what?" snapped the merchant. "I'm here on important business. Besides, I need all my money to get my new position."

The old man was shocked by the merchant's reply. He turned to some people who were also staying at the inn and said, "He used to be very poor himself. I supported him for ten whole years," the old man explained. "Then I loaned him money to start a business, and, as you see, he's grown very rich. I myself have suffered a hard life and lost all my money. I was hoping this merchant could repay me the money I gave him. Then I could pay my debts and return to my village."

After explaining this, the old man began to cry. The people in the crowd felt sorry for him, but the merchant acted like he hadn't heard a word the old man said.

Then a man stepped out of the crowd. "My name is Mr. Yang," he said. "Is the old man's story true?"

The merchant looked embarrassed, but replied, "Yes, I guess it is. But I don't have the money to repay him right now."

"Look," said Mr. Yang. "You're soon going to be a rich official, and you won't have any trouble borrowing money. If someone offered to lend you the money to repay the old man—interest-free—would you do it? You could repay the old man, and it wouldn't cost you anything."

"I suppose I could do that," the merchant grumbled.

"All right," said Mr. Yang. "If you sign this contract, I'll loan you the money to repay the old man." Everyone in the crowd nodded their heads in approval.

The deal was quickly done, and the money changed hands. The merchant put the money in his suitcase. The people in the crowd slowly went home, talking among themselves about how Mr. Yang had helped bring about a just resolution of the problem. The old man and Mr. Yang returned to their own villages.

After several more days in the city, the merchant was preparing to go home. But when he was packing his bags, he found that his money was gone! The locks had not been tampered with, so he couldn't even call the police. Then he knew that Mr. Yang was a clever magician and had tricked him.

VOCABULARY

KNOW THE SKILL: DENOTATION AND CONNOTATION

Words that mean almost the same thing can create different feelings. For example, one politician who will not change his beliefs might be described as firm, another as stubborn, and a third as pig-headed. The word *firm* creates a positive feeling of admiration for the politician's stand. The other two words, however, create negative feelings. The exact dictionary definition of a word is called its **denotation**. The meaning of a word that is created by a person's feelings about the word is its **connotation**.

DURING THE TEST

Think about the precise dictionary meaning of the word you are asked about. Then think of other words you have heard or used yourself with different connotations.

TEST EXAMPLE

1 Read this sentence from the selection. Then answer the question.
Then he knew that Mr. Yang was a clever magician and had tricked him.

What are some words with the same denotation as *tricked*, but with a more negative connotation?

_____

_____

THINK ABOUT THE ANSWER

Possible answers include *swindled*, *fooled*, *deceived*, *hoodwinked*, *duped*, *double-crossed*, and *hoaxed*. All of the these words have about the same meaning, or denotation, as *tricked*, but they have a negative connotation.

NOW YOU TRY IT

2 Look at the word below. Write a word with the same denotation, but a *negative* connotation. Then write a word with the same denotation, but a *positive* connotation.

Word	Negative Connotation	Positive Connotation
thin	_____	_____

Check your answer on page 109.

Review Your Work

If you finish the test before time is up, don't leave! Use every minute allowed to check your work. Make sure that you have answered all the questions. Check your answer sheet for mistakes. Proofread any writing. Double check the placement of decimal points and commas in numbers.

COMPREHENSION

KNOW THE SKILL: **MAKE PREDICTIONS**

Some test questions will ask you to make a prediction. The prediction may concern how a character in a story will act, or it may be about what might happen at the end of a story or after the story is over. Reading carefully is the key to making sound predictions.

DURING THE TEST

Keep on the lookout for clues an author may leave for you. For example, if a character in a story states firmly, "I would never, ever do something like that!" you shouldn't be surprised if the character does exactly that by the end of the story. Underline key words and phrases as you read. Then go back and look them over to help you predict the outcome.

TEST EXAMPLE

 What do you predict the merchant will do, now that he has learned that Mr. Yang tricked him? Explain your answer.

_____

_____

THINK ABOUT THE ANSWER

The merchant will probably go back home and do nothing. Reasons for this answer include he knew the people of the city were not on his side, he knew that he could not prove that Mr. Yang tricked him, and he knew that he had not treated the old man well and probably deserved what happened to him.

NOW YOU TRY IT

 Imagine you are the author of this story. What title would you use to give your readers help in predicting the outcome of the story?
    F   How Mr. Yang Tricked the Rich Merchant and Took His Money
    G   Going to the Capital City
    H   An Old Wrong Righted
    J   The Visit to the Inn

Check your answer on page 109.

Evidence, Please

Be sure to give reasons for an answer like the reasons given in the answer to question 1 above. You'll need to support your answer with evidence from the selection.

COMPREHENSION

KNOW THE SKILL: RELEVANT AND IRRELEVANT INFORMATION

Some information in a selection is **relevant**, or necessary to understanding the plot, characters, setting, or meaning. Other information is **irrelevant**, or not important or connected with these important elements of the selection. Tests may ask you to identify relevant and irrelevant information in a passage.

DURING THE TEST

As you read questions like the two below, eliminate answers that you feel are unnecessary, or irrelevant, to the issue in question. This will make it easier to choose the correct, relevant answers.

TEST EXAMPLE

1. What fact do you need to know to understand why the old man approached the merchant?
   - Ⓐ Mr. Yang was a clever magician.
   - Ⓑ He loaned the merchant money in the past.
   - Ⓒ There were other people staying at the same inn.
   - Ⓓ The merchant wanted to gain a new official position.

THINK ABOUT THE ANSWER

Option B is correct. The other options are irrelevant to why the old man approached the merchant. You need to know that he loaned the merchant money in the past to understand why he would approach him at the beginning of the story.

NOW YOU TRY IT

2. Which of the following sentences from the story tells relevant information about why the merchant went to the capital city?
   - Ⓕ To pay the bribe, he took with him a lot of money.
   - Ⓖ There once was a rich merchant from the town of Shansi.
   - Ⓗ "Then I loaned him money to start a business, and, as you see, he's grown very rich."
   - Ⓙ He went there to try to get an official position by bribing some important people.

Check your answer on page 109.

Don't Panic!
If you find that you are getting anxious before or during the test, take several slow, deep breaths to relax. Visualize being in a peaceful and calm place. Remind yourself that you are well prepared. Don't talk to other students before the test. Anxiety can be very contagious!

Read the newspaper editorial from the Hawkinsville Gazette. Then complete the activities on pages 18 through 20.

Let's Get Busy!

Since the dawn of history, people have gained many benefits from their nearness to rivers. Rivers offered irrigation, food, and safety. Today, the way we use rivers has changed, but their value has not. Our precious natural jewel, the Diamond River, has offered numerous benefits to Hawkinsville residents for over 150 years. Now, at the beginning of the twenty-first century, few benefits are more important than the recreation the Diamond provides. Boating, swimming, fishing, and other activities significantly improve the quality of life for all our citizens. Is there a single Hawkinsvillean who does not remember with fondness the river at dawn during spring or on a lazy summer afternoon? Who is not thrilled at the memory of the river covered with a crystal-clear coating of ice, which no doubt inspired its name many years ago?

Our city is fortunate to possess a terrific resource in the Diamond River. Unfortunately, we are perched on the brink of losing this valuable resource. Recent studies have shown an alarming 52% decline in certain key fish populations. Other government studies estimate that pollution and raw garbage flowing into the Diamond are threatening to turn its crystalclear waters into a cesspool of the rankest kind. Shockingly, for several weeks last summer, swimming in our beloved river was prohibited because of dangerously high levels of toxic substances in the water. This is a disgrace to Hawkinsville.

The time to begin the clean-up of the Diamond is now. We call on the Hawkinsville government to begin planning for the river's restoration. We encourage them to seek help from the state and federal governments. We challenge all citizens of Hawkinsville to accept the expense the clean-up will demand. To those who object to the cost of the river clean-up, we can only say that the cost of not restoring this priceless resource is greater by far. We all helped make the river sick. Therefore, we should all help to cure it.

Nature has given us the Diamond River. We now hold its future in our hands. We can choose to throw away this gift. Or we can make the effort now to restore it, thus preserving it for our fellow citizens and our children and grandchildren. The job won't be easy; fouling the river to this extent took many years. It may take a long time to reverse the damage. However, the sooner we begin this journey to a healthy river, the sooner we will all once again enjoy its many benefits.

Joe Worthington
Hawkinsville

Vocabulary

KNOW THE SKILL: TRANSITIONAL WORDS

Some test questions will ask you to identify transitional words. A **transitional word** or phrase is one that leads from one subject to another, or from a group of statements to a conclusion. Transitional words help writers create smooth and flowing passages. They can also signal to readers that a change in focus is coming. Some common transitional words are *therefore*, *thus*, *moreover*, *in comparison*, *on the other hand*, *likewise*, and *however*.

DURING THE TEST

Transitional words are often used together with semicolons or commas. They often occur in sentences at the beginning or end of paragraphs.

TEST EXAMPLE

1. Which passage contains a transitional word?
   - Ⓐ The job won't be easy; fouling the river to this extent took many years.
   - Ⓑ We all helped make the river sick. Therefore, we should all help to cure it.
   - Ⓒ Nature has given us the Diamond River. We now hold its future in our hands.
   - Ⓓ Since the dawn of history, people have gained many benefits from their nearness to rivers. Rivers offered irrigation, food, and safety.

THINK ABOUT THE ANSWER

Option B is correct. The transitional word is *therefore*, and it is used to signal a conclusion. Because everyone helped to make the river sick, the author concludes, everyone should help to cure it.

NOW YOU TRY IT

2. Write a comment about the editorial using a transitional word.

   _____

   _____

   _____

   Check your answer on page 109.

Use Only Test Information

Answer questions based on the information given. Do not use any outside personal information that you may have unless the questions asks you to.

COMPREHENSION

KNOW THE SKILL: **PERSUASIVE TECHNIQUES**

Persuasive writing attempts to convince people to agree with a position or take an action. Writers use different techniques to persuade readers. Among them are listing facts and examples, appealing to emotions, using colorful language, repeating key points, and anticipating and answering opposing viewpoints.

DURING THE TEST

As you read a piece of persuasive writing, ask yourself how you respond to different words and phrases. Is the writer trying to change your opinion or get you to take an action? How do the words accomplish these goals?

TEST EXAMPLE

1. Which paragraph uses the persuasive technique of listing facts and examples?
   - Ⓐ paragraph 1
   - Ⓑ paragraph 2
   - Ⓒ paragraph 3
   - Ⓓ paragraph 4

THINK ABOUT THE ANSWER

Option B is correct. In paragraph 2, the writer refers to recent studies of declining fish populations and increased garbage in the river.

NOW YOU TRY IT

2. Describe how the writer appeals to the reader's emotions in the editorial.

   _____
   _____
   _____
   _____

Check your answer on page 109.

Don't Rely on Your Memory

When answering questions about a reading passage, go back and re-read the passage. Don't rely on your memory. Skim the passage first, then read the questions. Finally, carefully read the passage, looking for the answer.

COMPREHENSION

KNOW THE SKILL: DISTINGUISH FACT AND OPINION

Test questions may ask you to differentiate between facts and opinions. **Facts** are things that can be proven. **Opinions** are things that people think. Persuasive writing will often contain statements of both facts and opinions. On tests, and in everyday life, it is important to be able to tell the difference between these two types of statements.

DURING THE TEST

Make sure you read all the answers before you choose one. Some of the answer options may be facts or opinions that are not in the passage. These answers are not correct. To be correct, the fact or opinion must be in the selection. When considering an answer, ask yourself if it might not be true. If it might not be true, then you know it is an opinion.

TEST EXAMPLE

1 Which of these statements is a fact?
- Ⓐ   This is a disgrace to Hawkinsville.
- Ⓑ   Our city is fortunate to possess a terrific resource in the Diamond River.
- Ⓒ   Since the dawn of history, people have gained many benefits from their nearness to rivers.
- Ⓓ   Boating, swimming, fishing, and other activities significantly improve the quality of life for all our citizens.

THINK ABOUT THE ANSWER

Option C is a fact because it can be shown to be true. Option A is an opinion because it cannot be proven and not all people would agree on what a disgrace is. Option B is also an opinion because some people may not feel that the city is fortunate to have the river. In the same way, option D is an opinion because not everyone feels that swimming, fishing, and other water sports significantly improve their quality of life.

NOW YOU TRY IT

2 Which of these sentences is an opinion?
- Ⓕ   Rivers offered irrigation, food, and safety.
- Ⓖ   The time to begin the clean-up of the Diamond is now.
- Ⓗ   Recent studies have shown an alarming 52% decline in certain key fish populations.
- Ⓙ   Shockingly, for several weeks last summer, swimming in our beloved river was prohibited because of dangerously high levels of toxic substances in the water.

Check your answer on page 109.

Read the poems by one of China's best-known poets. Then complete the activities on pages 22 and 23.

Two Poems by Li Bo (701–762 A.D.)

On a Quiet Night

I saw the moonlight before my couch,

And wondered if it were not the frost on the ground.

I raised my head and looked out on the mountain moon;

I bowed my head and thought of my far-off home.

Taking Leave of a Friend

Blue mountains to the north of the walls,

White river winding about them;

Here we must make separation

And go out through a thousand miles of dead grass.

Mind like a floating wide cloud,

Sunset like the parting of old acquaintances

Who bow over their clasped hands at a distance.

Our horses neigh to each other as we are departing.

Comprehension

KNOW THE SKILL: SETTING

The **setting** of a literary work is where and when it takes place. A story could take place on a ship at sea, in a medieval village, or in a home very much like your own. Where a story or poem is set contributes meaning to the work. Analyzing the setting can help you to better understand a work of literature.

DURING THE TEST

An author may not always tell you the setting of a story or poem. Look for clues about where it is taking place. For example, if the author tells you that the cries of sea gulls can be heard in the sky, then you know the setting has to be near the sea.

TEST EXAMPLE

1. Describe the setting of "On a Quiet Night."

   _____
   _____

THINK ABOUT THE ANSWER

You could have written a description like this: *The poem takes place at night, probably in a house somewhere in the mountains far away from the speaker's home.* You know the poem takes place at night because of the moon; the speaker mentions the mountain and also tells you that he is thinking of his far-off home.

NOW YOU TRY IT

2. Explain how the setting contributes to the mood of "On a Quiet Night."

   _____
   _____

Check your answer on page 109.

Stay Focused
Don't let anything distract you, especially other test-takers. Don't waste time looking out the window or at the other people in the room. You should have one focus and one focus only: the test!

COMPREHENSION

KNOW THE SKILL: POINT OF VIEW

A poem or story is told through the eyes of a certain person—from that person's point of view. The two points of view used most often in poems and stories are first person and third person. **First person** means that the narrator is a character in the poem or story. This person uses the pronouns *I, me, my,* and *mine* to describe the events. The reader learns this person's thoughts and feelings. **Third person** means that the story or poem is told by a narrator who is not part of the story. The narrator describes what happens and refers to the characters as *he, she,* and *they.* Readers might learn what several different characters think and feel.

DURING THE TEST

When identifying and analyzing the point of view of a text, ask yourself who is speaking. Who is telling the story? Through whose eyes do you see the events?

TEST EXAMPLE

1. From whose point of view is "Taking Leave of a Friend" told?
    - Ⓐ one of two people parting at sunset
    - Ⓑ two people standing on walls
    - Ⓒ a floating wide cloud
    - Ⓓ two horses neighing

THINK ABOUT THE ANSWER

Option A is correct. Although the author does not say so, he is one of the two friends standing together saying good-bye.

NOW YOU TRY IT

2. Is this poem written in the first person or the third person? Give reasons for your answer.

_____

_____

Check your answer on page 109.

Don't Waste Time

Don't waste time memorizing details from reading passages. Scan the questions to find out what you need to know, then answer the questions with the information you have. Some of the information in reading passages is not needed to answer the questions.

Graphic Information

KNOW THE SKILL: FORMS

Filling out applications, requests, questionnaires, and other types of forms is an important skill in school and everyday life. Tests may ask you to study and answer questions about forms.

DURING THE TEST

Begin by reviewing the form so you're sure you know what information is required. Then you will be prepared to answer the question.

TEST EXAMPLE

1 What important information does this application form NOT request?

- Ⓐ line for parent or guardian to sign if volunteer is under 18
- Ⓑ number of hours per month available for volunteer work
- Ⓒ what to do with the form after you have completed it
- Ⓓ All of the above

Hawkinsville Volunteer Information Form

Date _____
Name _____
Age _____
Address _____
_____

Telephone _____
E-mail _____
Previous Volunteer Experience _____
_____

Special Skills _____
_____

Thank you. We will contact you soon.

THINK ABOUT THE ANSWER

Option D is the answer. Each of these pieces of information should be included on an application form like this one.

NOW YOU TRY IT

2 Where on the form would you describe working at a children's summer drama camp? Explain your answer.

_____

_____

Check your answer on page 109.

All of the Above

If "All of the above" is an option, make sure that all the other options are correct before selecting it.

GRAPHIC INFORMATION

KNOW THE SKILL: **TABLES**

Many tests will ask you to read a table and answer questions based on the information the table provides. A **table** is a set of data organized in rows and columns. Tables are used as a way of organizing a lot of information in an easy-to-read format. Tables are especially useful for comparing numbers and amounts.

DURING THE TEST

Start by reading the title of the table and any information around the table. The table on this page compares the lengths of various world rivers.

TEST EXAMPLE

1. Which rivers empty into the Atlantic Ocean?
   - Ⓐ Congo and Niger
   - Ⓑ Amazon and Congo
   - Ⓒ Chang and Huang-He
   - Ⓓ Amazon and Mississippi-Missouri

Longest Rivers in the World

River	Location	Length (miles)	Outflow
Nile	Africa	4,160	Mediterranean
Amazon	South America	4,000	Atlantic
Chang (Yangtze)	China	3,964	East China Sea
Mississippi-Missouri	U.S.A.	3,710	Gulf of Mexico
Huang-He	China	3,395	Yellow Sea
Ob-Irtysh	Russia	3,362	Arctic Ocean
Congo	Africa	2,900	Atlantic
Lena	Russia	2,734	Laptev Sea
Mekong	Asia	2,700	South China Sea
Niger	Africa	2,500	Gulf of Guinea

THINK ABOUT THE ANSWER

Option B is correct. You can find this information by looking in the table's right-hand column, under the heading "Outflow."

NOW YOU TRY IT

2. How many world rivers are over 3,000 miles long?
   - Ⓕ 4
   - Ⓖ 5
   - Ⓗ 6
   - Ⓙ 7

Check your answer on page 109.

Guess the Answer

Before reading the possible options, guess the answer. Often you will find an answer that matches your guess.

GRAPHIC INFORMATION

KNOW THE SKILL: CHARTS

There are many different kinds of charts. One kind of chart that is especially useful for showing a procedure or process is called a flow chart. A **flow chart** is like a pathway that shows the different steps in a procedure. Just follow the pathway to find out the correct order of the steps.

DURING THE TEST

As with other charts, graphs, and maps, begin by reading the chart's title. Then examine the labels, notes, legend, and any other information that is provided. Use the information from the chart to eliminate incorrect answers and find the correct one.

TEST EXAMPLE

(1) Study the flow chart on this page. Then answer the question.

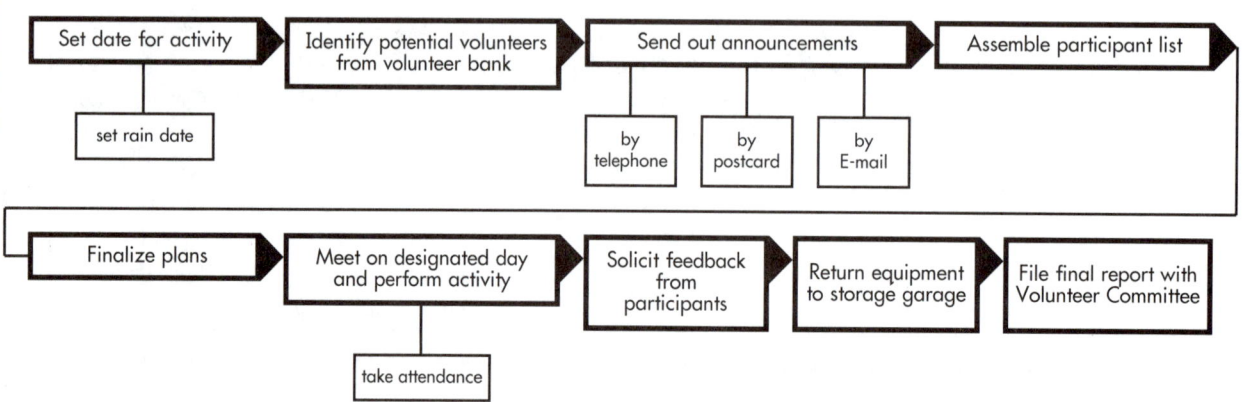

According to the chart, what are the available ways for contacting volunteers?

_____

THINK ABOUT THE ANSWER

There are three ways to contact volunteers: telephone, postcard, and E-mail. You can find this information listed as sub-steps under "Send out announcements."

NOW YOU TRY IT

(2) If you wanted to add a step for potential participants to confirm that they are going to attend the clean-up, where would you place it on the flow chart?

_____

_____

Check your answer on page 109.

GRAPHIC INFORMATION

KNOW THE SKILL: **MAPS**

On some tests you will be asked to read maps. You could be asked to give or follow directions based on a map, or find specific places, directions, routes, or distances.

DURING THE TEST

Begin by reviewing the map so you understand what it shows. Find the compass rose, key, scale, and other symbols that tell you what different symbols on the map mean. Notice which features are labeled.

TEST EXAMPLE

1. Shelley's class is meeting in the Riverside Park to clean up a stretch of the river bank. If she can walk 300 feet in 5 minutes, about how long will it take her to get to the park if she takes 1st Street to Maple Avenue?
    - Ⓐ about 60 minutes
    - Ⓑ about 45 minutes
    - Ⓒ about 27 minutes
    - Ⓓ about 15 minutes

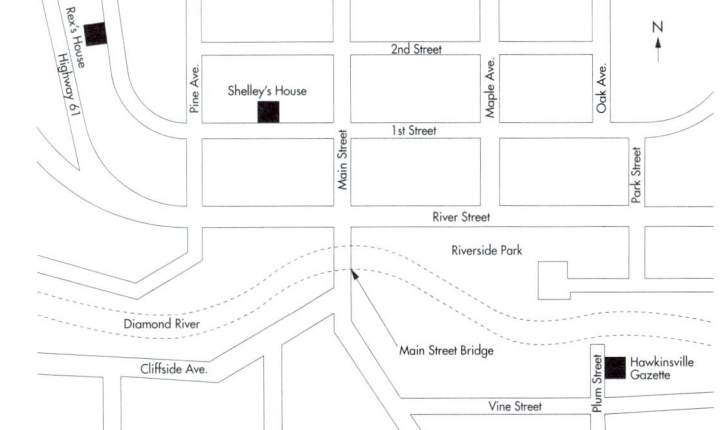

Scale

1,600 feet

THINK ABOUT THE ANSWER

Option C is the answer. To find it, measure the number of inches from Shelley's house to the park along her route (about 2 inches). Use the scale to determine the total number of feet she must walk (about 1,600). Divide 1,600 by 300 (the number of feet she can walk in 10 minutes) to get the number of 5-minute periods she will walk (5.3) Finally, multiply 5.3 x 5 minutes to get the total number of minutes her walk will take (26 2/3 minutes).

NOW YOU TRY IT

2. Write directions for how to get from the office of the Hawkinsville Gazette to Rex's house.

_____

_____

Check your answer on page 109.

REFERENCES

KNOW THE SKILL: TABLE OF CONTENTS

A **table of contents** shows the contents of a book arranged in order by chapter. The chapters usually have titles, and next to the chapter number and title is the page number on which the chapter begins. Often, some pages at the beginning of the book are in roman numerals. Most tables of contents also list sections at the end of the book, like the index, bibliography, and glossary.

DURING THE TEST

Read the question, then scan the table of contents quickly to find the information the test question requires.

TEST EXAMPLE

1. Where in this book would you look for a school report on the Mississippi River?
   - Ⓐ pages 116–122
   - Ⓑ page 69
   - Ⓒ pages 69–86
   - Ⓓ pages 69–85

```
Foreword, i
Introduction, iii
    1. A World of Rivers, 7
    2. River of the Pharaohs, 24
    3. Into the Heart of Africa, 40
    4. China's Mighty Rivers, 51
    5. Huck Finn's Favorite, 69
    6. From the Russian Heartland to the North Pole, 86
    7. Amazon, River of Mystery, 101
    8. Other Great Rivers, 116
    9. Can Our Rivers Survive? 123
Bibliography 138
Glossary 140
Index 142
```

THINK ABOUT THE ANSWER

The answer is option D. You can tell this chapter is about the Mississippi because Huck Finn floated down the Mississippi on his raft. Chapter 5 begins on page 69 and ends on page 85. You can tell that Chapter 5 ends on page 85 because Chapter 6 begins on page 86.

NOW YOU TRY IT

2. Do you think this book contains information about the Congo and Niger Rivers? In which chapter would you expect to find it? Explain your answer.

_____

_____

_____

Check your answer on page 109.

REFERENCES

KNOW THE SKILL: **DICTIONARY ENTRY**

A dictionary entry provides more than the correct spelling of a word. It also tells you how to pronounce and define the word. It offers the syllabication, part (or parts) of speech, and even synonyms, usage tips, and the history of the word. Knowing how to use a dictionary will help you on school assignments and in everyday life.

DURING THE TEST

When answering a test question about dictionary entries, first skim the entry. Next, read the question, which will tell you what information you're looking for in the entry. Then go back to the entry and choose the correct answer.

TEST EXAMPLE

Read the dictionary entry and answer the question.

es•tu•ar•y (ĕs' chōō-ĕr' ē) *n., pl.* **-ies**. 1. The part of the wide lower course of a river where its current meets the tides. 2. The part of an ocean or sea where it extends inland to meet the mouth of a river. [Latin *aesturarium*, from *aestus*, tide, surge, heat.]—esotuoaroioal (âr' ē-əi), *adj.*

1 Which word rhymes with the vowel in the first syllable of *estuary*?
- Ⓐ yes
- Ⓑ east
- Ⓒ taste
- Ⓓ this

THINK ABOUT THE ANSWER

Option A is the answer. *Yes*, with a *short e* sound, rhymes with the first syllable of *estuary*.

NOW YOU TRY IT

2 How is the word *estuary* related to its Latin roots?
_____
_____

Check your answer on page 109.

Don't Be Absurd!
Absurd choices are usually wrong. You can quickly rule them out.

Introduction to Writing

Understanding Writing Prompts

Many tests will ask you to write several paragraphs about a topic to see how well you write. You may be asked to write fiction or nonfiction. You might describe your thoughts or feelings, or you may have to explain how to do something.

The test will usually give you a topic to write about, called a writing prompt. A writing prompt can be a statement or a question. Here are some examples of writing prompts:

- Write about something you like or don't like, such as being the oldest, youngest, or only child in your family.
- Explain your opinion on a topic and give reasons to support it.
- Read a story, and then write another story like it.
- Read a story, and then predict what happens next or write about the characters.
- Write a letter or postcard as if you are on a trip to some place you always wanted to go.
- Explain a step-by-step procedure, like making popcorn, or how to do something, like riding a bicycle.
- Write about a memory, such as learning to ride a bike or your first bus ride.
- Write an informational essay about a topic.
- Write about a real or fictitious person you would like to invite to speak to your class.

Always read a writing prompt carefully so that you understand what you are supposed to do. Here are some general tips before you start writing:

- If you are asked to explain how to do something, put the steps in chronological order. Make sure you explain each step thoroughly.
- If you are asked to write nonfiction, include many details to support your main ideas.
- If you are asked to write a story, include characters with names.
- Give your story a beginning, a middle, and an end.
- Make sure the events in the story are in the correct order.
- Think through and plan every event carefully.
- Write a draft, read it, make any necessary changes, and rewrite it.
- Read your final draft carefully. Make sure that you followed all of the instructions in the writing prompt.
- Carefully check your spelling, punctuation, language usage, and grammar.
- Use good penmanship.

Understanding Scoring Rubrics

On most proficiency or standardized tests, someone will read your writing and use a rubric to score it. Many tests use a 4-point scoring rubric. The top score in each category is 4, while 0 is the lowest. Here is what a typical rubric looks like.

Scoring Rubric

Score	Content and Ideas	Organization	Sentence Structure and Clarity	Spelling, Punctuation, Usage, and Grammar
4	Excellent, well-developed ideas	Ideas are presented in a logical order	Sentences are complete and easy to understand	No more than two mistakes
3	Most ideas are well-developed	Most ideas are in a logical order	Most sentences are complete and easy to understand	No more than five mistakes
2	Some ideas do not relate to the topic or subject	Some ideas are in order	Some sentences are complete and easy to understand	No more than seven mistakes
1	Most ideas do not relate to the topic or subject	Few ideas are in order	Few sentences are complete and easy to understand	No more than ten mistakes
0	Little or no work completed	Little or no work completed	Little or no work completed	Little or no work completed

The person scoring your writing will give you a score for each category and then add the scores. In a rubric like this one, the highest score is 16.

To score well on the writing section of a test, you must make sure your writing exactly follows what the writing prompt asks you to do. Your ideas have to be carefully thought through. You must organize them in a way that makes sense and is easy for the reader to follow. You must write in complete, error-free sentences.

Brainstorm and Organize Your Ideas

When you are writing for a test, your time will be limited. You'll have to think clearly and quickly to organize your ideas. Graphic organizers, such as those below, can help you get started.

MAIN IDEA CHART

Your main ideas should be supported with details. This chart will help you organize your ideas and make sure you have details to back them up. You could make a chart for each main idea.

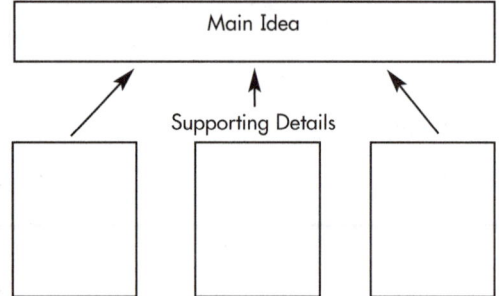

SEQUENCE CHART

A sequence chart is a good way to organize the steps in a procedure or the events in a story. Complete the chart and then write paragraphs about the topics in the order on the chart.

| event or step 1 |
| event or step 2 |
| event or step 3 |
| event or step 4 |
| event or step 5 |

STORY PLANNER

A story planner helps you to brainstorm the problem your characters will solve and how they will try to solve it.

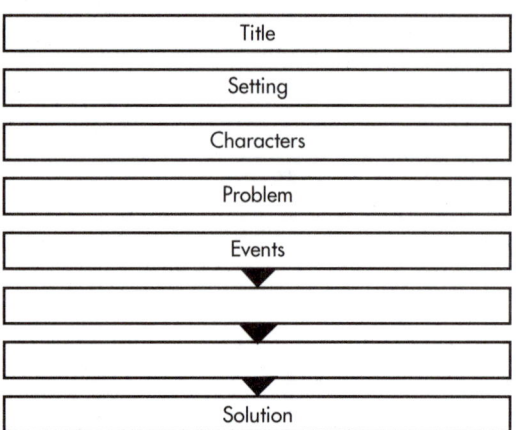

VENN DIAGRAM

If a writing prompt asks you to compare or contrast two or more things, a Venn diagram is a good way to organize likenesses (in the overlapping part) and differences (in the parts that do not overlap).

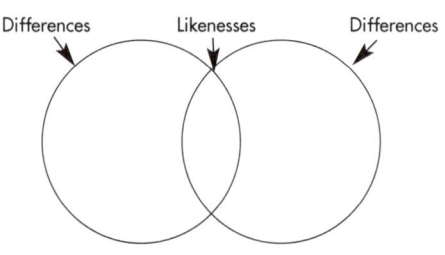

WRITING PROMPT

Most people are proud of where they live. They enjoy telling others about their community. Imagine you have been asked to write an introduction to your town or city for some visitors. What would you tell them? What details about your community would you include? Think about the things you like about your community. Is there anything you don't like? In what ways do you feel it is different from other towns and cities? Use this graphic organizer to help you get started planning and writing your first draft.

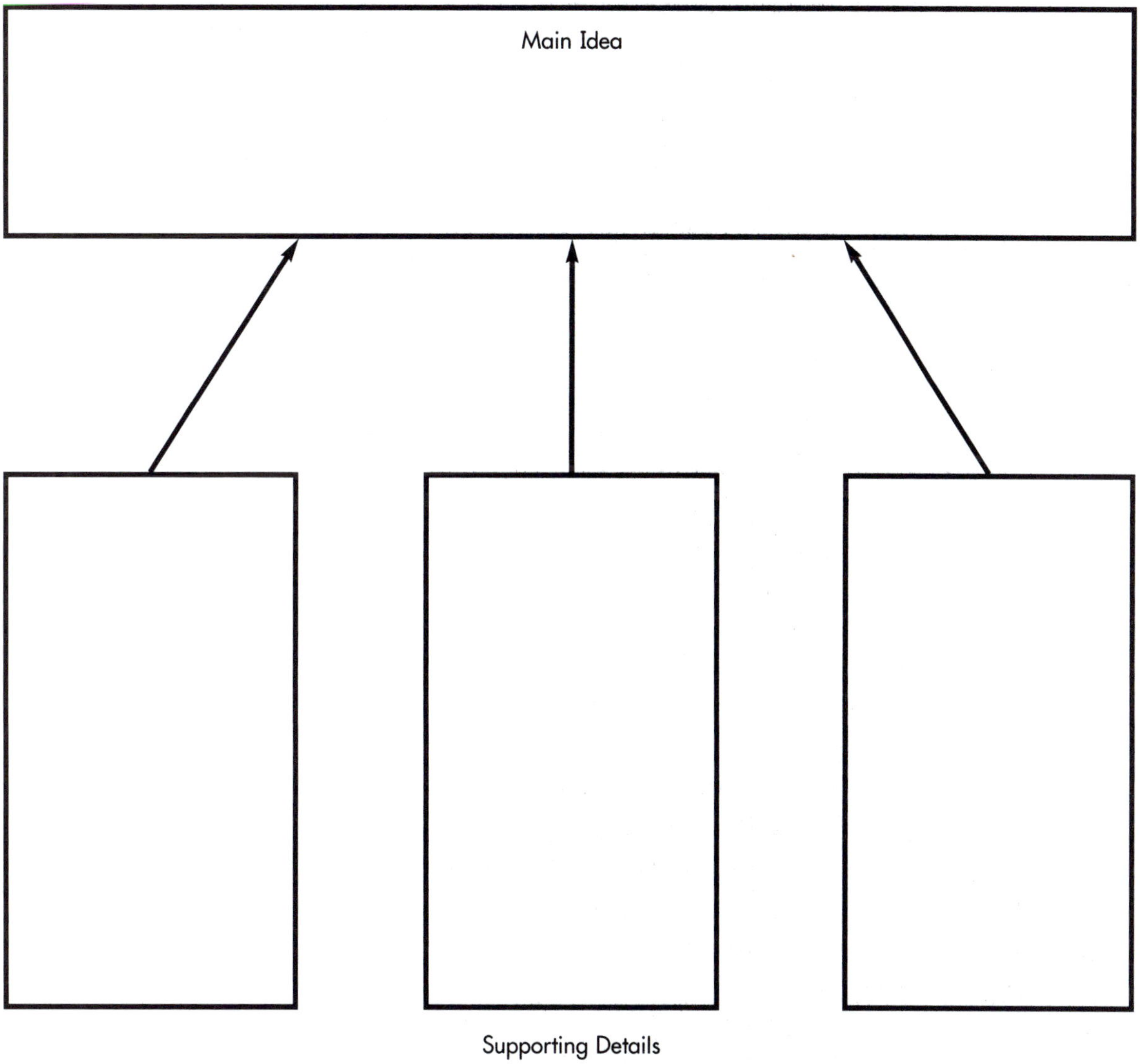

Main Idea

Supporting Details

PLAN AND WRITE YOUR FIRST DRAFT

Write your first draft on this page and the next.
Use separate sheets of paper if you need more room.

PLAN AND WRITE YOUR FIRST DRAFT

EDIT YOUR FIRST DRAFT

Between your first draft and your finished piece comes a very important step. It's when you take a good look at your writing and find ways to make it better. The step is called editing. It's not the same as writing, because you're not changing everything—just making what you have written better.

USING A CHECK LIST

Responding to a writing prompt like this one, maybe you notice that you haven't fully developed an important idea or forgotten a key detail, or that you've included too much unnecessary information. This writer's checklist can help you analyze your first draft and spot places you need to improve.

WRITER'S CHECKLIST

You will earn your best score if:

- ☐ you have included every piece of important information.
- ☐ you have not included unimportant things that the reader does not need to know.
- ☐ you have not repeated information unnecessarily.
- ☐ the details you include help the reader grasp the points you are making.
- ☐ your paragraphs are written in a logical order.
- ☐ readers can easily understand.
- ☐ your writing is lively and colorful.
- ☐ you make no spelling, grammar, punctuation, or capitalization errors.

Write Your Final Draft

Before you start your final draft, use the checklist on page 36 to review your first draft. Make sure you've covered the important points in the checklist, and look for other ways to improve the content, organization, clarity, and grammar of your first draft. Then write your final draft.

_____

_____

_____

_____

_____

_____

_____

_____

_____

_____

_____

_____

_____

_____

_____

_____

_____

Write Your Final Draft

Give Yourself a Score

_____
_____
_____
_____
_____
_____
_____

Go back to the writing rubric on page 31. Use the rubric to score your work. Give yourself a score from 4 to 0 for each category. Then ask someone else to score your writing. Compare and talk about the scores.

How I Scored It

Content and Ideas	Organization	Sentence Structure and Clarity	Spelling, Punctuation, Usage, and Grammar
_____	_____	_____	_____

How Someone Else Scored It

Content and Ideas	Organization	Sentence Structure and Clarity	Spelling, Punctuation, Usage, and Grammar
_____	_____	_____	_____

Introduction to Language

Few skills you can learn will be as valuable as your language skills. You communicate every day—in school, at home, at businesses, and with your friends—so it is important that you communicate clearly.

There are many different language skills. Some of the skills you can expect to see on tests are spelling, grammar, punctuation, sentence formation, and paragraph organization. Mastering these skills will not only help you do better on tests. These skills form the foundation for success in many other challenges you will meet in school and later life.

One of the best ways to improve your language skills is to read. Reading will sharpen your spelling skills and enlarge your vocabulary. Whenever you read, you learn how language is used. The more you read, the more reading will become an important part of your life.

Here is a list of key skills you will learn and practice in this section:

- Punctuation and Capitalization
- Hyphens
- Parentheses and Brackets
- Commas and Semicolons
- Infinitives and Participles
- Gerunds and Gerund Phrases
- Pronouns and Antecedents
- Parts of Speech
- Types of Sentences
- Lively Sentences
- Parallel Construction
- Coordination, Subordination, and Apposition
- Spelling

MECHANICS

KNOW THE SKILL: PUNCTUATION AND CAPITALIZATION

Every sentence must end with an end mark. Use a period to end a sentence that is a statement or command. Use a question mark for questions. Use an exclamation point for sentences that express strong emotion. Certain words must begin with a capital letter. These include the first word in a sentence; proper nouns and adjectives; the first letter of a direct quotation; and a word that takes the place of a person's name, such as *Mom* or *Grandpa*.

DURING THE TEST

Check to see if a noun or adjective refers to something or someone specific. If it does, it is proper and should begin with a capital letter. While reading each sentence, decide whether it is a statement, command, exclamation, or question. Then you'll know which end mark it needs.

TEST EXAMPLE

1. Choose the sentence that uses correct punctuation and capitalization.
   - Ⓐ Let's ask dad if he'll help us research World War I at the library.
   - Ⓑ Let's ask Dad if he'll help us research World War I at the Library.
   - Ⓒ Let's ask Dad if he'll help us research World War I at the library.
   - Ⓓ Let's ask Dad if he'll help us research world war I at the library?

THINK ABOUT THE ANSWER

The correct answer is C. *Let's*, the first word of the sentence, is capitalized, and *World War I*, a proper noun, is also capitalized. *Dad* is capitalized because it takes the place of the father's name. It ends with a period because it is declarative sentence. In option A, *dad* should be capitalized. In option B, *Library* should not be capitalized because it is not a proper noun. In option D, *World War I* should be capitalized, and the sentence should end with a period.

NOW YOU TRY IT

2. Choose the sentence that uses correct punctuation and capitalization.
   - Ⓕ My mom thinks Luigi's Ristorante serves the best Italian food in town.
   - Ⓖ My mom thinks Luigi's Ristorante serves the best Italian food in town?
   - Ⓗ My Mom thinks Luigi's Ristorante serves the best italian food in town.
   - Ⓙ My Mom thinks Luigi's Ristorante serves the best Italian food in Town.

Check your answer on page 109.

MECHANICS

KNOW THE SKILL: HYPHENS

Use a hyphen to join words that make up a single adjective, such as *hard-to-find* and *funny-looking*. Another use of the hyphen is in spelled-out compound numbers from twenty-one to ninety-nine. A third use of hyphens is in fractions when they are used as modifiers: *The song I'm writing is one-half completed.* Do not use a hyphen when a fraction is used as a noun: *Two thirds of the jewels are rubies.*

DURING THE TEST

As you read and write, keep in mind the ways hyphens are used. Don't confuse a hyphen (-) with a dash (—), which is longer and has different uses.

TEST EXAMPLE

1 Choose the sentence that is written correctly.
- Ⓐ Alex's grandfather is sixty four.
- Ⓑ Who was that good looking boy in the auditorium?
- Ⓒ Jarret bought a new book of easy to play guitar music.
- Ⓓ About one half of the team members played in the game.

THINK ABOUT THE ANSWER

Option D is correct. The fraction *one half* is used as a noun; therefore it should not be hyphenated. In option A, *sixty four* needs a hyphen. In option B, the words *good looking* make up a single adjective so they should be hyphenated. In option C, *easy to play* should be *easy-to-play* because the words make up a single adjective.

NOW YOU TRY IT

2 Choose the sentence that does NOT use hyphenation correctly.
- Ⓕ Dad left us with a bunch of ready-to-eat dinners when he left on a business trip.
- Ⓖ The Jaguars have won twenty-nine games in a row!
- Ⓗ Darcie's homework was three-fourths finished.
- Ⓙ One-third of my friends live on the south side.

Check your answer on page 110.

Use A Dictionary

Knowing which words to hyphenate and which words not to hyphenate can be tricky. The best guide is a dictionary. When in doubt, look up the word. Then you'll know how it should be treated when you see it on a test.

MECHANICS

KNOW THE SKILL: PARENTHESES AND BRACKETS

Parentheses enclose words that are apart from the main thought of a sentence. For example, *Janelle told me (I can't believe it!) she came in second in the lip-synch contest.* Include the correct end mark within the parentheses. Brackets are used to insert extra material in a quotation from another writer. For example, *"His [Walt Whitman's] most famous poem is probably* Song of Myself."

DURING THE TEST

Remember that parentheses can appear in many types of sentences. Brackets, however, usually appear only in a direct quotation with quotation marks.

TEST EXAMPLE

1 Which sentence is correct?
- Ⓐ That group's new CD [I didn't like the last one very well] is in the stores today.
- Ⓑ Your dog Midge looks awfully funny (when she's standing on her rear legs).
- Ⓒ What did you get (Don't worry, I won't tell anyone!) on the math test?
- Ⓓ The house I like the green one with white shutters is for sale.

THINK ABOUT THE ANSWER

Option C is correct. The words *Don't worry, I won't tell anyone!* are apart from the main thought of the sentence. Option A should use parentheses, not brackets, to enclose the words *I didn't like the last one very well.* In option B, *when she's standing on her rear legs* should not be in parentheses; it's an important part of the sentence, not apart from its meaning. In option D, *the green one with white shutters* should be in parentheses because it is apart from the main meaning of the sentence.

NOW YOU TRY IT

2 Which sentence is correct?
- Ⓕ The instructions stated, "Place part C [the wing-nut assembly] on the bolt."
- Ⓖ What was Brian [Is he crazy or what?] doing with that lampshade?
- Ⓗ Did she decide (which movie) Shawn prefers the first one to see?
- Ⓙ My older sister Wanida will be 12 (on her next birthday).

Check your answer on page 110.

"Overview" the Test

If it is allowed, quickly flip through the pages of the test so that you will know what lies ahead. This will help you plan your time. Ask whether you can write on the test. If you can, jot notes to yourself. Quickly judge how much time you will need for each part.

MECHANICS

KNOW THE SKILL: COMMAS AND SEMICOLONS

An **independent clause** has both a subject and a verb and can stand alone as a sentence. Many sentences join two independent clauses with a comma then a conjunction (*and, but, or, so, yet*) after the first independent clause. Two closely related independent clauses can also be joined by a semicolon. A **dependent clause** lacks a subject or a verb. Use a comma to set off a dependent clause when it begins a sentence. Also, use commas to set off an interruption in a sentence.

Correct: *Dogs are usually friendly, but cats can be standoffish.*
Correct: *Our dog is named Rufus; our cat is called Max.*
Correct: *Happy to be on my lap, Max purred softly.*
Correct: *No, Rufus, you can't come on our walk.*

DURING THE TEST

When you see a single sentence that includes two independent clauses, make sure that the sentence uses a comma and conjunction or a semicolon to join them.

TEST EXAMPLE

1 Which sentence is correct?
- Ⓐ Place the recyclables in the left bin; regular trash goes in the right bin.
- Ⓑ Be sure to wear your raincoat and don't forget to take an umbrella.
- Ⓒ Stunned by the last-minute victory; the team celebrated wildly.
- Ⓓ Hey Monique, you're wearing mismatched socks.

THINK ABOUT THE ANSWER

The answer is option A. The two independent clauses are joined with a semicolon. In option B, a comma belongs before *and* because *and* is the conjunction connecting the two independent clauses. In option C, a comma, not a semicolon, should follow *victory* because it is the last word of a dependent clause. In option D, there should be a comma before *Monique* to completely enclose the interruption in the sentence.

NOW YOU TRY IT

2 Which sentence is NOT correct?
- Ⓕ I'm talking to you, David, so please pay attention.
- Ⓖ Venus is closer to the sun than is Earth, but Mars is farther away.
- Ⓗ Mr. Ramirez is a good teacher; and Ms. Jackson is also very good.
- Ⓙ The catalog having arrived, I quickly turned to page 67 to see the sweaters.

Check your answer on page 110.

Grammar and Usage

KNOW THE SKILL: INFINITIVES AND PARTICIPLES

An **infinitive** is a form of a verb that usually begins with *to*. It is usually used as a noun. For example, *Victor hates to lose*. The infinitive is used as the direct object of the sentence and answers the question, What does Victor hate? A **participle** is another verb form that can be used as an adjective to modify a noun. A present participle ends in *-ing*. A past participle usually ends in *-ed*.

   Present participle: *Lying on my back, I gazed up at the clouds.*
   Past participle: *The house built by my uncle won an award.*

DURING THE TEST

Although the word *to* signals an infinitive, it is also used as a preposition: *Please give the box to Dad.* Check to see how *to* is used in the sentences you come across on tests. Not all words that end in *-ed* are past participles. Many are simply the past tense of a verb. For example, *Gabe watched the soccer game*. In the same way, many words that end in *-ing* are not present participles. They are the present progressive tense of a verb: *We are thinking of our friends.* Used this way, the *-ing* word will be preceded by *am*, *are*, *is*, *was*, *were*, or a contraction using these verbs.

TEST EXAMPLE

1. Which sentence does NOT correctly use an infinitive?
   - Ⓐ Does your sister like to play volleyball?
   - Ⓑ I want to find a new pair of running shoes.
   - Ⓒ To eat at that new restaurant is her greatest wish.
   - Ⓓ Mom and Dad are going to Myrtle Beach in the fall.

THINK ABOUT THE ANSWER

Option D is the answer. It does not contain an infinitive. In this sentence, the word *to* is a preposition, whose object is *Myrtle Beach*. In option A, the infinitive *to play* is used as a direct object. In option B, the infinitive *to find* is also used as a direct object. In option C, the infinitive *To eat* is used as the subject of the sentence.

NOW YOU TRY IT

2. Which sentence does NOT correctly use a present or past participle?
   - Ⓕ I was just thinking about what you said.
   - Ⓖ Rex decided to keep the camera ordered from the Internet.
   - Ⓗ Fastened with a rope to the dock, the boat did not float away.
   - Ⓙ Thinking she was late for the meeting, Melanie ran through the hallway.

Check your answer on page 110.

Grammar and Usage

KNOW THE SKILL: GERUNDS AND GERUND PHRASES

A **gerund** is a verb form that ends in *-ing* and is used like a noun. A gerund can be used as a subject: *Singing* takes practice. A gerund can also be used as an object: Do you enjoy *reading*? Gerunds usually occur in gerund phrases. **Gerund phrases** include a gerund and other words that modify the gerund. A gerund phrase can be used as a subject: *Singing in a choir* takes practice. A gerund phrase can also be used as a direct object: Many people like *reading mystery novels*.

DURING THE TEST

As you learned in the last lesson, some words ending in *-ing* are not gerunds. They can be present participles or present progressive verb tenses. Knowing how the *-ing* word is used will help you identify the correct answer.

TEST EXAMPLE

1. In which sentence is the gerund phrase underlined?
   - Ⓐ   Her family <u>is visiting her grandparents</u> in Texas.
   - Ⓑ   <u>Taking the bat in her hands</u>, Laura walked to plate.
   - Ⓒ   <u>Eating Chinese food</u> is sometimes a really messy job!
   - Ⓓ   My dad loves <u>listening</u> to CDs of music from the 1970s.

THINK ABOUT THE ANSWER

The correct answer is option C. The words *Eating Chinese food* are a gerund phrase used as the subject of the sentence. In option A, *is visiting her grandparents* is the verb and direct object of the sentence. In option B, *Taking the bat in her hands* is a present participle phrase that modifies *Laura*. In option D, *listening* is part of the gerund phrase used as the direct object; it should also be underlined.

NOW YOU TRY IT

2. In which sentence is the gerund phrase underlined?
   - Ⓕ   I enjoy <u>earning some extra money</u>.
   - Ⓖ   We noticed the man <u>standing on the corner</u>.
   - Ⓗ   Stopping <u>at the store to pick up a few things</u> is no big deal.
   - Ⓙ   <u>What were you thinking</u> when you decided to jump off the dock?

Check your answer on page 110.

Know What You're Answering
Read the question very carefully. Look for key words, such as *phrase* in the questions above, that will tell you exactly what answer the test requires.

Grammar and Usage

KNOW THE SKILL: PRONOUNS AND ANTECEDENTS

Pronouns are words that take the place of nouns, or that refer to nouns in a sentence. When a pronoun refers to a word in a sentence, that word is called the **antecedent**. An antecedent must agree with its pronoun in number (singular or plural) and gender (feminine, masculine, or neuter).

DURING THE TEST

Make sure you can identify the pronoun or antecedent in a sentence. If you are asked to provide a pronoun, knowing the antecedent will allow you to choose a pronoun that agrees in number and gender. If you are asked to provide an antecedent, knowing the pronoun will allow you to choose an antecedent that agrees in number and gender.

TEST EXAMPLE

1. Choose the answer that best completes the sentence.
   All students should report to _____ first-period classes on time.
   - Ⓐ her
   - Ⓑ his
   - Ⓒ its
   - Ⓓ their

THINK ABOUT THE ANSWER

Option D is correct. The third-person plural possessive pronoun *their* agrees in number with its antecedent, *students*. Option A, *its*, is singular. Options B and C are not possessive pronouns. They are, however, words that are often used incorrectly instead of *their*.

NOW YOU TRY IT

2. Choose the answer that best completes the sentence.
   If you see Tiffany at the library, please tell _____ about the overdue books.
   - Ⓕ it
   - Ⓖ she
   - Ⓗ her
   - Ⓙ them

Check your answer on page 110.

I Know This!

Knowing how a pronoun is used is the key to getting a question correct on a test. Review the different ways they are used as you prepare for a test.

Grammar and Usage

KNOW THE SKILL: PARTS OF SPEECH

There are eight kinds of words. They are called parts of speech. They include **nouns**, which name persons, places, things, or ideas; **pronouns**, which replace or refer to nouns; **verbs**, which show actions; **adjectives**, which modify nouns; **adverbs**, which modify verbs and adjectives; **prepositions**, which show relationships; **conjunctions**, which join parts of sentences; and **interjections**, which express strong feeling. You may be asked to identify any of these parts of speech.

DURING THE TEST

Look for clues to identifying parts of speech. Nouns are often preceded by the words *the*, *a*, or *an*. Verbs usually follow nouns and have common verb endings such as *-s*, *-ed*, and *-ing*. Adjectives often end in *-ish*, *-y*, or *-ful*. Many adverbs end in *-ly*. Be careful, though. Verbs can end in *-s*, but so can plural nouns.

TEST EXAMPLE

 Which sentence does NOT contain an adverb?
- Ⓐ You'll succeed eventually.
- Ⓑ The loud boom echoed across the countryside.
- Ⓒ I often wonder if I will be accepted into the program.
- Ⓓ Run quickly and tell them about the attack on the fort!

THINK ABOUT THE ANSWER

Option B is correct. It does not contain an adverb. The word *loud* is an adjective that modifies *boom*. In Option A, the adverb *eventually* modifies the verb *succeed*, telling how you will succeed. In option C, the adverb *often* modifies *wonder*, telling how the subject wonders. In option D, the adverb *quickly* modifies the verb *run*, telling how the person addressed should run.

NOW YOU TRY IT

 Write an adjective that completes the sentence.
Climbing a high mountain is one of the most _____ feats in the world.

Check your answer on page 110.

Talk to Your Teacher
Ask your teacher to talk about any problems you have had with tests in the past. Your teacher might know things that will help you. He or she might have advice that can help you get through difficult parts of the test.

SENTENCE STRUCTURE

KNOW THE SKILL: TYPES OF SENTENCES

There are four types of sentences: declarative, interrogative, imperative, and exclamatory. Each has a different purpose. A **declarative** sentence makes a statement or expresses a fact. It ends with a period. An **interrogative** sentence asks a question and ends with a question mark. An **imperative** sentence expresses a command or request. It often ends with a period. If it expresses strong emotion, it can end with an exclamation point. An **exclamatory** sentence expresses surprise or strong emotion and ends with an exclamation point.

DURING THE TEST

Remember that imperative sentences usually omit the subject, which is often understood to be *you*. Exclamatory sentences often omit the verb. Interrogative sentences often place part of the verb before the subject. Declarative sentences, however, usually follow subject-verb-object order.

TEST EXAMPLE

1. Which of the following is an imperative sentence?
   - A Call me when you get home, Brandi
   - B Are you going to call me when you get home
   - C When I got home, I heard the telephone ringing
   - D Why didn't you answer the phone when it started ringing

THINK ABOUT THE ANSWER

The answer is option A. It gives a command and should be followed by a period. Option B is an interrogative sentence and should be followed by a question mark. Option C is a declarative sentence and should be followed by a period. Option D is an interrogative sentence and should be followed by a question mark.

NOW YOU TRY IT

2. Which of the following is NOT an interrogative sentence and should not end with a question mark?
   - F Is that your bike?
   - G How much is twenty times sixteen?
   - H Where I live is none of your business?
   - J Would Michael like to join us for lunch?

Check your answer on page 110.

Watch for Certain Words

Keep an eye out for words such as *but*, *not*, and *except*. These words place limits on the answer. Also watch out for absolute words such as *always*, *never*, and *only*. If one of these words is in a question, it means there can be no exceptions.

SENTENCE STRUCTURE

KNOW THE SKILL: LIVELY SENTENCES

Changing the length and structure of your sentences can keep them lively and interesting. Too many of the same kinds of sentences can be boring. Try to mix short and longer sentences. Use simple, compound, and complex sentences. Also, begin your sentences in different ways.

DURING THE TEST

If you are asked to rewrite sentences so that they are more varied and lively, begin by analyzing the pattern of the sentences given. Do they all begin with the subject, followed by the verb? Are they all short and choppy? Do they repeat words unnecessarily? This will help you to identify how to improve the sentences.

TEST EXAMPLE

1 Read this paragraph. Then, combine the first two sentences in a way that will add variety and liveliness to the paragraph.

> Saturday turned out to be a perfect day for a hike. Saturday was a perfect spring day, with sunny skies and a soft breeze. Fluffy white clouds were in the sky. The clouds moved across the blue sky. The clouds reminded me of young lambs in a pasture. We walked through the gorge at the state park. We saw wildflowers and we saw many colorful birds. The birds were gathering twigs and making nests. The birds were flitting from branch to branch.

_____

_____

THINK ABOUT THE ANSWER

You could have written something like this: *With sunny skies and a soft breeze, Saturday turned out to be a perfect spring day for a hike.* The problem with the paragraph is that all the sentences begin with the subject, followed by a verb. The sentences are also all about the same length. The rewritten sentence begins with an adjective phrase and is longer.

NOW YOU TRY IT

2 Combine the third, fourth, and fifth sentences in a way that will add variety and liveliness to the paragraph.

_____

_____

Check your answer on page 110.

SENTENCE STRUCTURE

KNOW THE SKILL: PARALLEL CONSTRUCTION

Sentences in which equal thoughts are expressed in grammatically equal ways are said to use **parallel construction**. Here are some examples:

Parallel	Not Parallel
• I like to kick a soccer ball and to shoot baskets. (both are infinitives) • I like kicking a soccer ball and shooting baskets. (both are gerunds)	• I like kicking a soccer ball and to shoot baskets. (*kicking* is a gerund; *to shoot* is an infinitive)

DURING THE TEST

Try to find elements in the sentence that are equal, like those in the examples above. These are elements that need to be treated in the same way grammatically in order for the sentence to express parallel construction.

TEST EXAMPLE

1. Which sentence correctly uses parallel construction?
   - Ⓐ Our choices are to give up and continuing to fight.
   - Ⓑ To eat dinner now or waiting until they arrive is our problem.
   - Ⓒ Walking on the beach and swimming in the ocean are delightful.
   - Ⓓ My grandparents enjoy both water skiing and to play bridge with their friends.

THINK ABOUT THE ANSWER

Option C is correct. Both parts of the compound subject are in the same grammatical form (gerund phrases). In option A, *to give up* is an infinitive and *continuing to fight* is a gerund. In option B, *to eat dinner now* is an infinitive and *waiting until they arrive* is a gerund. In option D, *water skiing* is a gerund and *to play bridge* is an infinitive.

NOW YOU TRY IT

2. Which sentence does NOT use parallel construction correctly?
   - Ⓕ Birds fly, fish swim, and snakes wriggle.
   - Ⓖ Call your cousins or send them an E-mail.
   - Ⓗ Devin doesn't like waiting in line and filling out applications.
   - Ⓙ Bratwursts can be fried, broiled, or you can grill them on a barbecue.

Check your answer on page 110.

SENTENCE STRUCTURE

KNOW THE SKILL: COORDINATION, SUBORDINATION, AND APPOSITION

Coordination, subordination, and apposition allow you to vary sentences and link ideas in different ways. **Coordination** is the linking of ideas that are equally important. **Subordination** is the linking of more important ideas with less important ideas. An **appositive** is a noun, sometimes with modifiers, that is placed next to a noun or pronoun to add more information or identify it. In these examples, the subordinate information and the appositive are underlined:

Coordination: *Dress in layers when you go hiking, or you may be uncomfortably hot.*
Subordination: *Jimmy Carter, who was born in Georgia, was elected president in 1976.*
Apposition: *Ontario, the smallest of the Great Lakes, is also the easternmost.*

DURING THE TEST

Certain words can give clues about how ideas are linked. Words that often signal coordination are *and, or, but, as a result, so, because, however, for example*, and *therefore*. Words that often show subordination are *who, whose, which, that, when*, and *where*.

TEST EXAMPLE

1. Which sentence uses subordination to link more important and less important ideas?
   - Ⓐ I hope Haley arrives soon so she can help us build the model of the steam engine.
   - Ⓑ Belgians and Percherons are huge, while Shetland ponies are much smaller.
   - Ⓒ Seat belts definitely save lives, but some people still do not wear them.
   - Ⓓ Barky, whose collar was lost in the woods, is my dog.

THINK ABOUT THE ANSWER

The answer is option D. The less important information, *whose collar was lost in the woods*, is subordinated to the more important information, *is my dog*. In all the other options equally important information is linked through coordination.

NOW YOU TRY IT

2. Which sentence contains an appositive?
   - Ⓕ The county fair begins in July and runs into August.
   - Ⓖ The Amazon, the world's second-longest river, begins in Peru.
   - Ⓗ My aunt, whom you've never met, will be visiting us next week.
   - Ⓙ Chess, which is a challenging game, may have been invented in India.

Check your answer on page 110.

Spelling

KNOW THE SKILL: INFLECTED ENDINGS

Many words change their spelling when endings are added. Some common endings, or inflections, that can cause spelling trouble, are *-able, -ly, -ful, -ing, -ness, -y,* and *-ed*. Learn the rules for these inflections. When spelling many words that end in *y*, preceded by a consonant, change the *y* to an *i* when you add *-ed* or *-s* to the end of the word. When spelling one-syllable words, double the final consonant when you add *-ed* or *-ing* to the end of the word.

DURING THE TEST

Try to think of a word that is spelled in a similar way to the one on the test. The test word probably adds an inflection in the same way. For example, *logically* adds an *l* to *logical*, just like *finally* adds an *l* to *final*.

TEST EXAMPLE

1. Choose the option with the correct spelling to complete the sentence.
   The dog shelter was filled with the barking of several dozen _____ .
   - Ⓐ pupies
   - Ⓑ puppys
   - Ⓒ puppies
   - Ⓓ puppeys

THINK ABOUT THE ANSWER

Option C is correct. The spelling of *puppies* follows the rule described above, change the *y* to an *i* when you add *-s* to the end of the word.

NOW YOU TRY IT

2. Choose the option with the correct spelling to complete the sentence.
   Halfway through the race, Paul complained that he was _____ tired.
   - Ⓕ getng
   - Ⓖ geting
   - Ⓗ getting
   - Ⓙ geeting

Check your answer on page 110.

Keep Things In Perspective

Remember that it's just a test! There are many measures of achievement, and test scores are just one of them.

SPELLING

KNOW THE SKILL: FREQUENTLY MISSPELLED WORDS

Tests will ask you to identify misspelled words. There's no shortcut to being a good speller. The two keys are reading a lot and practicing spelling.

DURING THE TEST

Spelling rules, like the ones you learned in the last lesson, can help you on some questions. At other times, however, you'll be on your own. That's when your hours of reading and practicing will pay off. Remember to think of a word that is similar to the one on the test—the two words may be spelled the same way. Another aid is to pronounce the word; this may keep you from adding extra letters or leaving letters out.

TEST EXAMPLE

 Look at the underlined words. Which is spelled correctly?
- Ⓐ Dina was really <u>surprised</u> when we jumped up and yelled "Happy Birthday!"
- Ⓑ Have you been to the new store that sells <u>athaletic</u> gear?
- Ⓒ The army suffered a <u>disasterous</u> defeat.
- Ⓓ Our new kitten is totally <u>irresistable</u>.

THINK ABOUT THE ANSWER

The answer is option A. It is spelled correctly. The correct spelling in option B is *athletic*. The correct spelling in option C is *disastrous*. The correct spelling in option D is *irresistible*.

NOW YOU TRY IT

 Look at the underlined words. Which is spelled incorrectly?
- Ⓕ Mr. Gomez was <u>grateful</u> for the gift.
- Ⓖ Can you tell me when the accident <u>occurred</u>?
- Ⓗ The <u>temperture</u> reached 100 degrees yesterday.
- Ⓙ My mom is thinking about getting a TV <u>satellite</u> dish.

Check your answer on page 110.

Read, Read, Read!
The best way to learn to spell is to read lots of different things. Books, magazines, and newspapers will let you see lots of words that are spelled correctly. The more you read, the better speller you'll become!

Introduction to Math

You will use your math skills in school, at work, and in everyday life. Understanding mathematics will also help you to solve problems, think logically, and apply abstract reasoning. Most standardized tests feature a math section that asks you to apply a variety of skills. This section of this workbook will help you sharpen your math skills and get you ready to do well on tests. Here is a list of key skills you will learn and practice in this section:

- Compare and Order Integers and Fractions
- Convert Decimals to Scientific Notation
- Add and Subtract Numbers Written in Scientific Notation
- Add and Subtract Fractions with Unlike Denominators
- Multiply Integers
- Divide Decimals
- Check the Reasonableness of an Answer
- Least Common Denominator
- Find Ratios
- Volume of a Solid
- Solve Problems Involving Scale Factors
- Solve Problems Involving Rates
- Pythagorean Relationship
- Congruence and Similarity
- Examine Shapes on a Coordinate Grid
- Evaluate Expressions
- Solve Equations with Two Variables
- Graph Linear Equations
- Find Measures of Center and Spread
- Compute Probabilities for Simple Compound Events
- Represent Data Graphically
- Solve a Multi-Step Problem
- Solve a Proportion Problem

Number Sense and Numeration

KNOW THE SKILL: COMPARE AND ORDER INTEGERS AND FRACTIONS

Compare and place integers in order by comparing digits from left to right until they are different. Use the symbols equals (=), less than (<), and greater than (>) in expressions. Compare and place fractions in order by first converting them to fractions with like denominators. Then compare numerators; the fraction with the smaller numerator is smaller. For both integers and fractions, a negative number is always less than a positive number.

DURING THE TEST

A way to remember what the "greater than" and "less than" symbols mean is that the "point" of the angle always points toward the smaller number. In the expression 6 < 8, the point is toward the 6, the smaller number. In 12 > 9, the point of the angle is toward 9.

TEST EXAMPLE

1. Which group of numbers is written in order from greatest to least?
   - Ⓐ 445,485; 454,845; 544,584
   - Ⓑ 32; 19; -40
   - Ⓒ 1/4; 1/3; 1/2
   - Ⓓ -6; 2; 1

THINK ABOUT THE ANSWER

The answer is option B. Comparing digits from left to right, you find that the 3 in 32 is greater than the 1 in 19. Therefore, the first number is greater than the second number. The third number is a negative number, so it is always smaller than positive numbers. In option A, the correct order, found by comparing digits, is 544,584; 454,845; 445,485. In option C, the correct order, after converting the fractions is 1/2 (6/12); 1/3 (4/12); 1/4 (3/12). In option D. the correct order is 2; 1; -6.

NOW YOU TRY IT

2. Which number correctly completes the expression?

   _____ > 12
   - Ⓕ 13
   - Ⓖ 11
   - Ⓗ 1/2
   - Ⓙ -21

Check your answer on page 110.

Advantage Test Prep Grade 8 © 2005 Creative Teaching Press

Number Sense and Numeration

KNOW THE SKILL: CONVERT DECIMALS TO SCIENTIFIC NOTATION

Very large or very small numbers are sometimes written in **scientific notation**. Scientific notation uses negative exponents of 10, multiplied by a smaller number (called the base), to represent very small numbers. For example, 0.00000032 can be written as 3.2×10^{-7}. The decimal point has been moved seven places to the left. 3.2×10^{-7} means the same thing as $3.2 \times 0.1 \times 0.1 \times 0.1 \times 0.1 \times 0.1 \times 0.1 \times 0.1$.

DURING THE TEST

When converting a number from scientific notation to standard notation, remember to move the decimal point to the right or left the same number of places as the exponent. For negative exponents, move the decimal point to the left. For positive exponents, move the exponent to the right.

TEST EXAMPLE

1. $7.6 \times 10^{-6} =$
   - Ⓐ   0.00076
   - Ⓑ   0.000076
   - Ⓒ   0.0000076
   - Ⓓ   0.00000076

THINK ABOUT THE ANSWER

The answer is option C. 7.6×10^{-6} means you must multiply 7.6 times 0.1 six times. Doing this gives you an answer of .0000076. Notice the answer has five zeros following the decimal point.

NOW YOU TRY IT

2. $4.5 \times 10^{-8} =$ _____
   - Ⓕ   0.0000000045
   - Ⓖ   0.000000045
   - Ⓗ   0.00000045
   - Ⓙ   0.0000045

Check your answer on page 110.

It Can't Hurt!
You may want to count the number of decimal places twice—just to make sure you've got the right number.

Advantage Test Prep Grade 8 © 2005 Creative Teaching Press

NUMBER SENSE AND NUMERATION

KNOW THE SKILL: ADD AND SUBTRACT NUMBERS WRITTEN IN SCIENTIFIC NOTATION

When you add or subtract numbers written in scientific notation, you must first change the numbers so that they are both expressed in the same power of 10. Then you add or subtract the bases and convert the answer to standard scientific notation, with the base as a whole number and decimal.

DURING THE TEST

To solve this problem, $3.7 \times 10^6 + 2.3 \times 10^4$, first convert the numbers to the same power of 10, in this case 10^4. Do this by moving the decimal in the base, one place for each difference in the power of 10: $3.7 \times 10^6 = 370.0 \times 10^4$. The problem then becomes to add $2.3 \times 10^4 + 370.0 \times 10^4$. The answer is 372.3×10^4. It is necessary to write the final answer in standard scientific notation. Therefore, move the decimal in the base two places to the left and raise the power of 10 by 2. The correct answer is 3.723×10^6. The procedure is the same for subtraction.

TEST EXAMPLE

1) $4.5 \times 10^6 + 6.8 \times 10^3 = $ _____

    Ⓐ $4,506.8 \times 10^3$
    Ⓑ 4.5068×10^3
    Ⓒ 45.068×10^6
    Ⓓ 4.5068×10^6

THINK ABOUT THE ANSWER

The correct answer is option D. Here's how to find it: Convert the first number to a base times 10^3 by moving the decimal in the base three places to the right. This gives a problem of $4,500.0 \times 10^3 + 6.8 \times 10^3 = 4,506.8 \times 10^3$. Then, convert the answer to a whole number and a decimal, which leaves a correct final answer of 4.5068×10^6.

NOW YOU TRY IT

2) $9.1 \times 10^5 - 3.6 \times 10^4 = $ _____

    Ⓕ 87.4×10^4 Ⓗ 87.4×10^5
    Ⓖ 8.74×10^5 Ⓙ 8.74×10^4

Check your answer on page 110.

Read the Directions Carefully

This is a no-brainer! Pay attention while you read the directions. It will help you avoid careless errors.

COMPUTATION AND OPERATIONS

KNOW THE SKILL: ADD AND SUBTRACT FRACTIONS WITH UNLIKE DENOMINATORS

In order to add and subtract fractions, the denominators must be the same. To add or subtract fractions with unlike denominators, rewrite them so that they have like denominators. To do this, use the least common denominator (LCD). For example, to add 1/6 and 2/7, you must use the LCD 42. Multiply both the numerator and denominator of 1/6 by 7, and the numerator and denominator of 2/7 by 6. This gives you equivalent fractions with like denominators, 7/42 and 12/42. Then add the numerators to get the answer, 19/42.

DURING THE TEST

Remember that you need to rewrite fractions with unlike denominators using the LCD. Then simplify your answer, if necessary.

TEST EXAMPLE

 5/6 + 3/5 = _____
- Ⓐ 1 13/30
- Ⓑ 43/30
- Ⓒ 1 1/3
- Ⓓ 8/11

THINK ABOUT THE ANSWER

The answer is option A. The LCD for 6 and 5 is 30. Multiply the numerator and denominator of 5/6 times 5 and the numerator and denominator of 3/5 times 6 to get fractions with like denominators of 30 (25/30 and 18/30). Then add the numerators to get 43/30, or 1-13/30.

NOW YOU TRY IT

 7/8 − 1/3 = _____
- Ⓕ 2
- Ⓖ 3/4
- Ⓗ 13/24
- Ⓙ 29/24

Check your answer on page 110.

Check This Out

Check your answer to an addition problem by subtracting one of the addends from the sum. You should get the other addend. Check your answer to a subtraction problem by adding the difference to the number that you subtracted.

COMPUTATION AND OPERATIONS

KNOW THE SKILL: MULTIPLY INTEGERS

Integers are also known as positive and negative numbers. Multiplying two positive numbers gives you a positive number product:

14 x 12 = 168

Multiplying two negative numbers also gives you a positive number product:

-14 x (-12) = 168

Multiplying a positive and a negative number gives you a negative number product:

14 x (-12) = -168

DURING THE TEST

Keep these rules in mind when you are multiplying integers:

If the signs are the same the product is positive.

If the signs are different the product is negative.

TEST EXAMPLE

 -32 x (-13) = _____
- Ⓐ 19
- Ⓑ -19
- Ⓒ 416
- Ⓓ -416

THINK ABOUT THE ANSWER

The correct answer is option C. The product of 32 and 13 is 416. Because both numbers have the same sign (negative), the product is a positive number.

NOW YOU TRY IT

 24 x (-35) = _____
- Ⓕ -840
- Ⓖ 840
- Ⓗ -59
- Ⓙ 59

Check your answer on page 111.

Trust Your Instincts

If you have a hunch about an answer, it is more likely to be the correct answer. Don't second guess your decisions and change your answers unless you have a very good reason to believe you made a mistake.

Computation and Operations

KNOW THE SKILL: DIVIDE DECIMALS

Dividing decimals is just like dividing whole numbers. The only difference is you must place the decimal correctly. When dividing a decimal by a decimal, move the decimal point in the divisor all the way to the right. Count the number of places the decimal point moved. Then move the decimal point of the dividend the same number of places to the right. Now divide by a whole number.

DURING THE TEST

When you are dividing a decimal by a whole number, don't forget to place the decimal point in the quotient right above the decimal point in the dividend.

TEST EXAMPLE

1. 0.639 ÷ 2.47 = _____
   - Ⓐ 2,587
   - Ⓑ 25.87
   - Ⓒ 2.587
   - Ⓓ 0.2587

THINK ABOUT THE ANSWER

The correct answer is option D. Did you remember to move the decimal point in both the dividend and divisor two places to the right and add a zero as a place holder after the last digit in the dividend? The problem then becomes 639 ÷ 2,470 = 0.2587.

NOW YOU TRY IT

2. 19.202 ÷ 0.529 = _____
   - Ⓕ 0.36299
   - Ⓖ 3.6299
   - Ⓗ 36.299
   - Ⓙ 362.99

Check your answer on page 111.

Get the Point

On math questions like these, make sure you always double check the placement of decimal points in numbers.

Estimation and Number Theory

KNOW THE SKILL: CHECK THE REASONABLENESS OF AN ANSWER

It sometimes happens, in life and on tests, that you need to know at a glance if the information you find is reasonable. Does it make sense, or is it obviously off the wall? One good way to check if your answers to math questions are reasonable is to estimate before solving. Here are some ways you can use estimating to check the reasonableness of your answers:

- Round numbers to estimate sums, differences, products, and quotients.
- Use front-end estimation to estimate sums and differences.
- Use compatible numbers to estimate sums, differences, products, and quotients.

DURING THE TEST

When you need to estimate or predict an answer on a test:
- Read the problem carefully to decide which operation you need to use.
- Choose a suitable estimation method.
- Estimate the answer.
- Eliminate choices that are not close to the estimate.
- Finally, solve to find the right answer.

TEST EXAMPLE

1. Which of the following is a reasonable estimation of the answer to this multiplication problem: 1/4 x 612?
   - Ⓐ 15
   - Ⓑ 1.5
   - Ⓒ 150
   - Ⓓ 1,500

THINK ABOUT THE ANSWER

The correct answer is option C. You know that 1/4 of 60 is about 15, by using a technique called compatible numbers. Therefore, because 600 is ten times greater than 60, your estimated answer is ten times greater than 15, or 150. The actual answer is 153.

NOW YOU TRY IT

2. Which of the following is a reasonable estimation of the answer to this division problem: 7,414 ÷ 289.6?
   - Ⓕ 2.5
   - Ⓖ 25
   - Ⓗ 250
   - Ⓙ 0.25

Check your answer on page 111.

Estimation and Number Theory

KNOW THE SKILL: LEAST COMMON DENOMINATOR

In order to perform operations with fractions, all the fractions must have the same denominator. This number is called the **least common denominator** (LCD). The LCD is the lowest common multiple of two or more denominators.

DURING THE TEST

Another way to think of the LCD is the smallest number that can be evenly divided by all the numbers in the set. For example, the smallest number that can be evenly divided by 3, 4, and 5 is 60 (60 ÷ 3 = 20, 60 ÷ 4 = 15, and 60 ÷ 5 = 12).

TEST EXAMPLE

1. The least common denominator of 6, 9, and 12 is _____.
    - Ⓐ 72
    - Ⓑ 36
    - Ⓒ 6
    - Ⓓ 3

THINK ABOUT THE ANSWER

Option B is correct. 36 is the smallest number that can be divided evenly by 6, 9, and 12. You would need to find this number to solve a problem like 1/6 + 2/9 + 7/12 = _____.

NOW YOU TRY IT

2. 144 is the least common denominator of _____.
    - Ⓕ 9, 12, and 18
    - Ⓖ 8, 14, and 24
    - Ⓗ 14 and 36
    - Ⓙ 24 and 56

Check your answer on page 111.

Study With a Group

Form a small study group with members of your class. You can prepare for tests together. After tests you can brainstorm new preparation strategies as a group.

Estimation and Number Theory

KNOW THE SKILL: FIND RATIOS

A **ratio** is a representation of the relationship between two numbers. For example, the ration of 24 to 40 is 3:5. A ratio can be written in different ways; 3:5, 3/5, and 3 to 5 are all ways to write ratios. Each one states that the first number has the same relationship to the second number as 3 to 5.

DURING THE TEST

To determine the ratio of two numbers, divide both numbers by the greatest common factor. The GCF is the largest number that is a common factor of two or more numbers. For example, the greatest common factor of 24 and 40 is 8. If you are asked to find the ratio of 24 to 40, divide each number of the ratio by the GCF of 8. The answer is a ratio of 3:5.

TEST EXAMPLE

1 Which of the following pairs does NOT represent a ratio of 5:8?
- Ⓐ 10:16
- Ⓑ 15:24
- Ⓒ 20:32
- Ⓓ 30:42

THINK ABOUT THE ANSWER

The answer is option D. 30:42 represents a ratio of 5:7. Find this by dividing each term by the GCF of 6 (30 ÷ 6 = 5 and 42 ÷ 6 = 7). The GCFs of the other options are A (2), B (3), and C (4).

NOW YOU TRY IT

2 What is the ratio of 63:49?
- Ⓕ 6:4
- Ⓗ 9:7
- Ⓖ 7:9
- Ⓙ 3:2

Check your answer on page 111.

Don't Get Stuck!
Sometimes you'll come across a tricky question. Don't let it worry you. Reread the question, then try to solve it. If you find yourself stumped, circle the question and move on. You can come back to it later. If you still don't know the answer, review your options and make the best guess you can.

MEASUREMENT

KNOW THE SKILL: VOLUME OF A SOLID

The volume of a figure is the measurement of the space inside it. You will need to memorize these formulas for finding the volumes of different solids. The answers are always in cubic units.

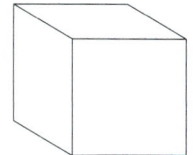

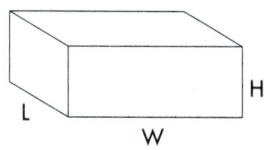

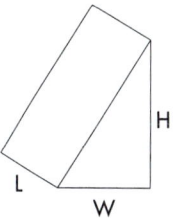

DURING THE TEST

If a drawing is not provided, you may want to do a quick sketch of the solid on scratch paper. You can write in the values given to help you better see the figure you want to find the volume for.

TEST EXAMPLE

1 What is the volume of this solid?

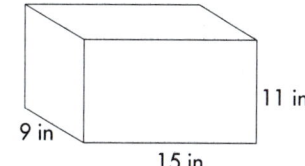

- Ⓐ 2,970 in³
- Ⓑ 1,485 in³
- Ⓒ 70 in³
- Ⓓ 35 in³

THINK ABOUT THE ANSWER

Option B is correct. This solid is a rectangular prism. Inserting the measurements of the solid into the correct formula ($v = lwh$) gives the equation $1,485 = 11 \times 15 \times 9$.

NOW YOU TRY IT

2 What is the volume of this solid?

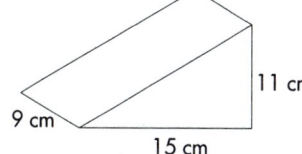

- Ⓕ 25 cm³
- Ⓖ 50 cm³
- Ⓗ 270 cm³
- Ⓙ 540 cm³

Check your answer on page 111.

Be Prepared!

If you show up prepared, you will be better able to focus. Arrive early, and make sure to bring everything you need. Bring pencils and pens, some paper, and a calculator and dictionary, if allowed. Wear a watch so you can keep track of time. If your watch beeps, turn the sound off.

MEASUREMENT

KNOW THE SKILL: **SOLVE PROBLEMS INVOLVING SCALE FACTORS**

A **scale** is a kind of ratio used on maps, drawings, models, and other kinds of representations. A scale shows the ratio of the drawing to the actual thing it represents. For example, a map of your state might have a scale of 1 inch = 25 miles. This means 1 inch on the map is equal to 25 miles of your state. A small model of a car might have a scale of 1 inch = 3 feet. This means that one inch of the model is equal to 3 feet of the real car.

DURING THE TEST

Look first for the explanation of the scale used in the question. This is your key to answering any scale question correctly.

TEST EXAMPLE

1 On a map of New Brunswick, Canada, the scale is 1 centimeter = 20 kilometers. How far is it from Moncton to Saint John if the two cities are 7.5 centimeters apart on the map?

- Ⓐ 7.5 kilometers
- Ⓑ 20 kilometers
- Ⓒ 12 kilometers
- Ⓓ 150 kilometers

THINK ABOUT THE ANSWER

The correct answer is option D. To find it, multiply the number of kilometers that one centimeter represents times the total number of centimeters between the two cities on the map: 7.5 x 20 km = 150 km.

NOW YOU TRY IT

2 Imagine you were going to create a scale drawing of your bedroom at home to fit on a piece of 8 1/2 x 11 inch notebook paper. Which scale would be most appropriate for your drawing?

- Ⓕ 1/2 inch = 1 foot
- Ⓖ 1/2 inch = 1 inch
- Ⓗ 1 inch = 10 feet
- Ⓙ 2 inches = 1 foot

Check your answer on page 111.

Use the Process of Elimination

First rule out answers that you know are wrong. Then rule out answers that are partly wrong or don't seem to fit. If two options are very similar they might both be incorrect. This process will narrow down possible answers.

Measurement

KNOW THE SKILL: SOLVE PROBLEMS INVOLVING RATES

Many tests will ask you to solve math problems that involve rates. **Rates** include how fast, how much, and how often something happens. How many miles will a car travel at a certain rate of speed? How much money will someone earn at a certain rate of pay? How long will a job take at a certain rate of performance?

DURING THE TEST

Always make sure you keep the different numbers in a rate problem clear. Make notes to separate rate of speed from miles traveled, or rate of pay from hours worked. This will also help you to know the kind of unit the answer must contain, for example, hours rather than miles, or years rather than dollars.

TEST EXAMPLE

1. Edgar and his family are driving to visit his grandparents. The trip is 400 miles. If the car will average 60 miles an hour, with an hour for lunch and rest stops, how much total time will the trip take?

   Ⓐ 7 hours, 40 minutes   Ⓒ 6 hours, 40 minutes
   Ⓑ 7 hours, 20 minutes   Ⓓ 6 hours

THINK ABOUT THE ANSWER

The correct answer is option A. This problem has several steps. First divide the total number of miles the trip includes by the number of miles they will average each hour: 400 ÷ 60 = 6.667, or 6 2/3 hours. Because an hour consists of 60 minutes, 2/3 of an hour is equal to 40 minutes. Then, to this 6 hours, 40 minutes, you need to add an extra hour, which the family will use for lunch and rest stops. The total trip will take 7 hours, 40 minutes.

NOW YOU TRY IT

2. Calvin has invested his savings of $750 in an account that pays 3% simple interest per year. How much money will he have at the end of the year if he does not withdraw any of his savings?

   Ⓕ $22.50   Ⓗ $772.50
   Ⓖ $750.00   Ⓙ $775.20

   Check your answer on page 111.

Work Quickly

Plan your time, and work quickly through each section of the test. Do not linger on a section if you are done with it. Move on to the next section. Work quickly, but not so quickly that you make mistakes.

Geometry

KNOW THE SKILL: PYTHAGOREAN RELATIONSHIP

A triangle is a figure with three sides. When one of the angles of a triangle is a right, or 90°, angle, the triangle is called a right triangle. The sides of a right triangle are usually referred to as *a*, *b*, and *c*. The side called *c*, which is the side opposite the right angle, is always the longest. Another name for this longest side is the *hypotenuse*. A formula for finding the lengths of the three sides of a right triangle is:

$a^2 + b^2 = c^2$

This formula is known as the Pythagorean Theorem.

DURING THE TEST

Always look for the right angle symbol in a triangle. That way, you'll know you're dealing with a right triangle and also which side is the hypotenuse.

TEST EXAMPLE

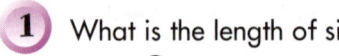

1. What is the length of side *b* in this triangle?
   - Ⓐ 10 in
   - Ⓑ 7 in
   - Ⓒ 6 in
   - Ⓓ 8 in

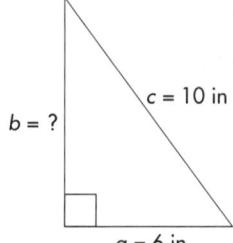

THINK ABOUT THE ANSWER

The correct answer is option D. To find it, use the values of 6 for *a* and 10 for *c* in the Pythagorean Theorem. The equation becomes $6^2 + b^2 = 10^2$, or $36 + b^2 = 100$. Solve the equation for b^2 by subtracting 36 from each side. This leaves $b^2 = 64$. The square root of 64 is 8, the length of side *b*.

NOW YOU TRY IT

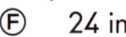

2. What is the length of a straight line drawn from point B to point C in this rectangle?
   - Ⓕ 24 in
   - Ⓖ 15 in
   - Ⓗ 12 in
   - Ⓙ 11 in

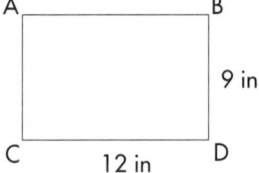

Check your answer on page 111.

Don't Prepare at the Last Minute

Give yourself time to relax before the test. Studying up to the last minute will cause you to be tense. Trying to learn new things right before the test might cause you to be confused about things you already know. Having a healthy relaxed attitude will help you handle the task coolly and confidently.

GEOMETRY

KNOW THE SKILL: **CONGRUENCE AND SIMILARITY**

When two figures are **congruent**, they have the same size and shape. The corresponding sides and the corresponding angles are congruent. When two figures are **similar**, they have the same shape, but not necessarily the same size. The corresponding sides are in proportion, and the corresponding angles are congruent.

DURING THE TEST

A test may ask you to identify congruent or similar triangles or other polygons. You may also be asked to select corresponding angles or sides of congruent or similar figures.

TEST EXAMPLE

1 Which pair of figures is NOT congruent?

 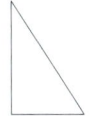   

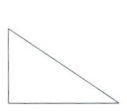   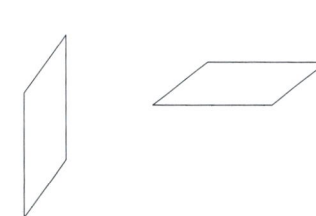

THINK ABOUT THE ANSWER

The answer is option D. These two polygons are similar, but not congruent. All the other pairs are the same size and shape.

NOW YOU TRY IT

2 These figures are similar. Which angle corresponds to angle C?
- Ⓕ angle X
- Ⓖ angle Y
- Ⓗ angle Z
- Ⓙ None of the above

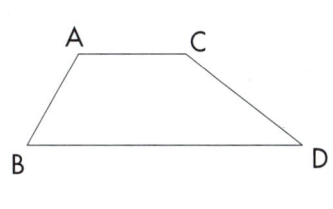
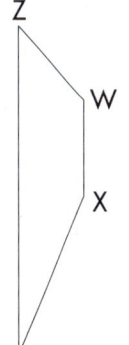

Check your answer on page 111.

Geometry

KNOW THE SKILL: EXAMINE SHAPES ON A COORDINATE GRID

Slides, flips, and turns are ways that shapes can be moved on a coordinate grid. These movements are also known as **transformations**. The form and size of the shape does not change—only the position of the shapes changes.

DURING THE TEST

Keep these definitions in mind:
- A **slide** (also called a *translation*) is the motion of a shape along a line. You can think of the way a drawer opens. The position of the drawer changes, but its shape does not.
- In a **flip** (also called a *reflection*), a shape takes on the shape of its own reflection across a line. Think of the lower-case letters *b* and *d*. When a *d* is flipped, it looks like a *b*.
- In a **turn** (also called a *rotation*), a shape is rotated around a single point. If a *d* is rotated around the point at the top of the part that sticks up so that it is upside-down, it will look like a *p*.
- In a **dilation**, the shape of the figure remains the same, but the size changes. A figure that is similar to another has been dilated.

Shapes are often drawn on a grid, making it easier to work with transformations. A test may ask you to slide, flip, or turn a shape drawn on a grid.

TEST EXAMPLE

1 If this shape is slid along line BC, what will it look like?

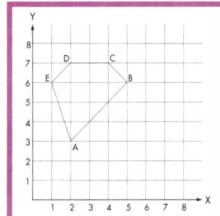 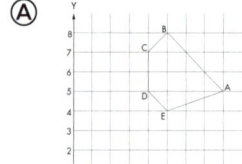 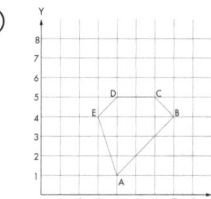 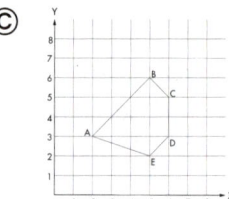

THINK ABOUT THE ANSWER

The answer is option B. It has been slid along line BC. Option A has been rotated around point A. Option C has been flipped across line AB.

NOW YOU TRY IT

2 If this shape is flipped over line JI, what will it look like?

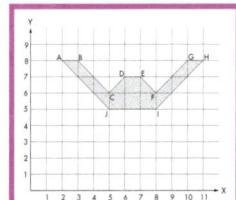 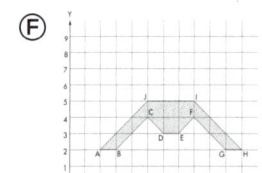 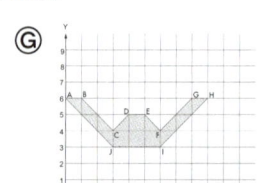 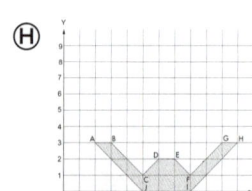

Check your answer on page 111.

ALGEBRAIC THINKING

KNOW THE SKILL: EVALUATE EXPRESSIONS

In an expression or equation, letters can stand for unknown numbers. These letters are known as **variables**. When we replace a variable with a specific number and then perform the operations, it is called **evaluating the expression**. To evaluate the expression $3x + (x - 1)$, where $x = 3$, begin by replacing each letter with its assigned value:

$3(3) + (3 - 1)$

Then do the operations, first multiplying, then subtracting:

$9 + (2) = 11$

DURING THE TEST

Always do math operations in the following order: First, do operations inside parentheses. Next, clear the exponents. Then, perform all multiplications and divisions from left to right. Finally, do all additions and subtractions from left to right.

TEST EXAMPLE

1 What is the value of the expression $(2n \div 4)n$ if $n = 8$?
- Ⓐ 32
- Ⓑ 16
- Ⓒ 8
- Ⓓ 4

THINK ABOUT THE ANSWER

The correct answer is option A. Here's how to evaluate this expression when $n = 8$: $(2 \times 8 \div 4) \times 8 = (16 \div 4) \times 8 = (4) \times 8 = 32$.

NOW YOU TRY IT

2 What is the value of the expression $3x - (x + 2)$ if $x = 4$?
- Ⓕ 4
- Ⓖ 6
- Ⓗ 9
- Ⓙ 12

Check your answer on page 111.

What Does That Mean?

Think about the meanings of words if you forget the meaning of a math term. For example, if you can't remember what the math term *variable* means, think about the word in another context. In weather, winds can be "light and variable." In this sentence, *variable* means changing. In math a variable is a symbol that can have changing values.

Algebraic Thinking

KNOW THE SKILL: SOLVE EQUATIONS WITH TWO VARIABLES

An **equation** is a mathematical sentence that shows that two expressions are equal. An equation often has one or more variables in it. The solution to an equation with two variables is a pair of numbers. When the first number of the pair is equal to one variable in the equation, the second number of the pair must be equal to the second variable.

DURING THE TEST

You may be asked to find the value of a pair of variables in an equation. The simplest way to solve an equation with two variables is substitution. Assign a value to one of the variables. Then solve the equation to find the value of the other variable. Find the value of the remaining unknown variable by using inverse operations. Addition and subtraction are inverse operations. Multiplication and division are inverse operations.

TEST EXAMPLE

1. Which pair of values solves the equation $2x + 4y = 20$?
   - Ⓐ 2, 4
   - Ⓑ 2, 2
   - Ⓒ 4, 8
   - Ⓓ 2, 6

THINK ABOUT THE ANSWER

The correct pair is option A. Solve this equation by assigning the first value of the pair to x and the second value to y. That makes the equation $(2 \times 2) + (4 \times 4) = 4 + 16 = 20$. None of the other pairs equal 20.

NOW YOU TRY IT

2. What is the value of x in this equation if $y = 3$?
   $6x \div 2 = 3y$
   - Ⓕ 2
   - Ⓖ 3
   - Ⓗ 4
   - Ⓙ 5

Check your answer on page 111.

Check It Out
Always check your answer by replacing the value you find for the variable in the original equation.

ALGEBRAIC THINKING

KNOW THE SKILL: GRAPH LINEAR EQUATIONS

The value of variables in an equation can be shown on a graph. The graph consists of two crossed lines called axes. The x-axis is horizontal. The y-axis is vertical. Each axis has a scale, usually 1, 2, 3, 4, and so on. The point where they meet has a value of 0,0. This means zero on the horizontal x-axis and zero on the vertical y-axis. A point on the graph represents a value for each variable. A linear equation is an equation whose solution is a straight line on the graph.

The graph to the right shows the line for the equation $3x - y = 2$. Can you see that each point on the line represents a pair of values that will correctly solve the equation?

DURING THE TEST

To find points on a graph that will solve an equation, start by assigning a value to the x, then solve to find the value of y. Find this point. Assign the next higher value to x and solve again. This will give you another point. Because the equation is linear, a straight line drawn through these two points will give you a set of points, each of which will solve the equation.

TEST EXAMPLE

1 Which equation does the graph show?

Ⓐ $x = 2y$ Ⓒ $x = y + 1$
Ⓑ $2x = y$ Ⓓ $x = y \div 2$

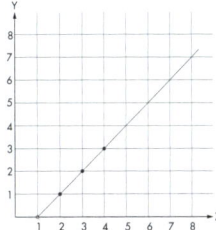

THINK ABOUT THE ANSWER

Option C is correct. Replacing the variables in the equation with the values represented by the points correctly solves the equation. For example, the first set of points is 1, 0 (that is, $x = 2$ and $y = 1$). These values give you an equation of $1 = 0 + 1$. The second set of numbers gives an equation of $2 = 1 + 1$, and so on.

NOW YOU TRY IT

2 Which graph shows the equation $3x = y$?

Ⓕ 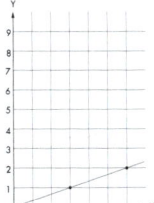   Ⓖ 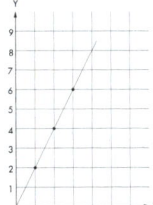   Ⓗ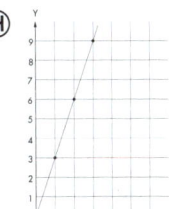

Check your answer on page 111.

Data Analysis and Probability

KNOW THE SKILL: FIND MEASURES OF CENTER AND SPREAD

A **measure of center** is a value at the center of a set of data. There are different ways to find the center of a data set.

- The most common is the **mean**. Many people call the mean an average. To find the mean, add all the values in the data set. Then divide the sum by the number of values.
- Another measure of center is the **median**. To find the median, arrange all the data points in order. The value in the middle is the median.
- The **mode** is the value that occurs most often.

The difference between the two greatest values in a data set is called the **range**. The range is a measure of spread.

DURING THE TEST

Tests may ask you to find any of these measures of center or spread. Make sure you know which one you're being asked to calculate.

TEST EXAMPLE

1 Hawk Patrol of Scout Troop 261 has nine members. The number of merit badges earned by the members are 12, 3, 5, 0, 1, 6, 13, 8, and 11. What is the patrol's mean number of merit badges per member, rounded to the nearest whole number?

- Ⓐ 5
- Ⓑ 6
- Ⓒ 7
- Ⓓ 9

THINK ABOUT THE ANSWER

The correct answer is option C. To calculate the mean, find the total of all the merit badges (59) and divide by 9, for an answer of 6.555. Round the answer up to 7.

NOW YOU TRY IT

2 The low temperatures during one winter week were 4, 9, 23, 25, 19, 14, and 12 degrees. What was the range of the temperatures?

- Ⓕ 25
- Ⓖ 21
- Ⓗ 15
- Ⓙ 14

Check your answer on page 111.

Step by Step
When using more than one operation to solve a problem, such as adding the values in a data set, then dividing by the number of values, work in steps. Do one operation at a time.

Data Analysis and Probability

KNOW THE SKILL: COMPUTE PROBABILITIES FOR SIMPLE COMPOUND EVENTS

Probability is the chance that an event will happen. For example, if you flip a coin, what are the chances you will get heads? You can compute the probability of this event happening this way:

$$\frac{\text{Successful outcomes (getting heads)}}{\text{All possible outcomes (getting heads or tails)}} = \frac{1}{2}$$

The probability of getting heads is 1/2. Probability is expressed as a fraction. 1 means that an event is certain to happen, while 0 means that an event is certain not to happen. The probability of getting either a heads or a tails is 1. The probability of getting neither a heads nor a tails is 0, since one or the other has to happen.

DURING THE TEST

You may be asked to compute the probability of two events happening. This is called a **compound event**. For example, what is the probability of flipping two coins and getting two heads? Find the probability of a compound event this way:
- Find the probability of one event happening (getting 1 heads) = 1/2
- Find the probability of the other event happening (getting 1 heads) = 1/2
- Multiply the two fractions that represent the probability of each event happening
  1/2 x 1/2 = 1/4

The probability of flipping two coins and getting heads on both flips is 1/4.

TEST EXAMPLE

1. A game spinner is divided into 7 equal sections: orange, tan, red, yellow, green, blue, and brown. What is the probability that you will get a tan and then a blue on two consecutive spins?
   - Ⓐ 1/49
   - Ⓑ 2/49
   - Ⓒ 2/7
   - Ⓓ 1/7

THINK ABOUT THE ANSWER

The answer is option A. To find it, compute the probability for getting a tan on your first spin (1/7). Then find the probability for getting a blue on your second spin (also 1/7). Multiply the two probabilities (1/7 x 1/7) to get 1/49. These are the chances that you will get a tan and a blue on consecutive spins.

NOW YOU TRY IT

2. A single die has 6 sides. If you throw a pair of dice while playing a board game, what is the probability that you will get a 12?
   - Ⓕ 1/6
   - Ⓖ 1/12
   - Ⓗ 2/12
   - Ⓙ 1/36

Check your answer on page 111.

Data Analysis and Probability

KNOW THE SKILL: REPRESENT DATA GRAPHICALLY

It is often easier and clearer to represent data in a graph, rather than in words. A **graph** is a drawing that shows how different numbers relate to each other. For example, think of a histogram. A **histogram** is a bar graph that shows the relative sizes of different sets of data. A larger or taller column or bar represents a higher value or number of the things being compared than a smaller one.

DURING THE TEST

Remember how different kinds of graphs show relationships. A pie chart, in which a circle is divided in different size "pieces of pie" that show different amounts or values. It is good for showing how parts relate to a whole. A line graph can show how values change over time, such as how the average daily temperature goes up and down over a month.

TEST EXAMPLE

1. Look at this pie chart. It shows the number of students in one class who chose different sports as their favorite. What percentage of the class chose basketball as their favorite sport?
    - Ⓐ 7%
    - Ⓑ 25%
    - Ⓒ 28%
    - Ⓓ 33%

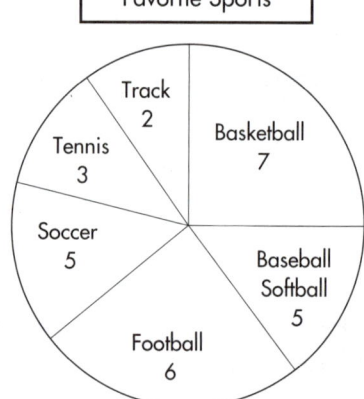

THINK ABOUT THE ANSWER

The correct answer is option B. To find it, you must first find the total number of students in the class by adding up the number of votes each sport received: 28 in all. Basketball received 7 of the 28 votes, or 7/28, simplified to 1/4 or 25%. The pie chart also gives you a visual indication of this part. The "pie slice" for basketball takes up 1/4 of the total "pie."

NOW YOU TRY IT

2. Which of the following combinations of sports were the favorites of half the class?
    - Ⓕ baseball/softball, basketball, and track
    - Ⓖ soccer, track, and tennis
    - Ⓗ soccer, football, and tennis
    - Ⓙ basketball and football

Check your answer on page 111.

Problem Solving

KNOW THE SKILL: SOLVE A MULTI-STEP PROBLEM

Follow these steps to decide how to solve a word problem:
1. Read the problem carefully.
2. Analyze the information given.
3. Make a plan for solving the problem.
4. Do the math and check your answer.

DURING THE TEST

Tests may ask you to solve problems that involve more than one step to finding the correct answer. The two problems on this page are examples of multi-step problems. You may find it helpful to write on scratch paper to make clear the parts of the problem.

TEST EXAMPLE

1. Devin wants to buy an encyclopedia CD-ROM. Its regular price is $129.95. For a short time, it is available for 15% off. What is the encyclopedia's price with the discount?
   - Ⓐ $114.95
   - Ⓑ $110.46
   - Ⓒ $99.95
   - Ⓓ $19.49

THINK ABOUT THE ANSWER

The answer is option B. To find the answer in this multi-step problem, you must first determine the amount of money a 15% discount represents. Multiply the original price times 0.15 (15%) to get $19.49. Then you must subtract the amount Devin gets off the regular price from the regular price to find the new price, minus his discount: $129.95 – $19.49 = $110.46.

NOW YOU TRY IT

2. Carla and Ming ordered these items on the menu when they went out to lunch: two Caesar salads at $8.95 each, one soft drink at $1.25 and one bottled water at $1.50, a piece of chocolate cake for $2.50, and a bowl of ice cream for $1.85. If they want to tip the waiter 15%, how much will their total cost for the meal be?
   - Ⓕ $21.80
   - Ⓖ $23.65
   - Ⓗ $25.00
   - Ⓙ $28.75

Check your answer on page 111.

Step by Step
You may want to write down the steps at the top of this page for solving multi-step problems when you come to a section of story problems. That way, you'll remind yourself what you need to do to solve the problems.

Problem Solving

KNOW THE SKILL: SOLVE A PROPORTION PROBLEM

A **ratio** is a representation of the relationship between two numbers. The two numbers are usually separated by a colon. An example is 2:3. This ratio can also be written 2/3. Either way, we say the ratio is "two to three." A proportion is an equation with a ratio on each side.

DURING THE TEST

A test may ask you to find an unknown number in one of the ratios of a proportion. Often you will have to set up the equation from a story problem. Use cross products to find the missing number, a procedure known as solving a proportion. For example, here's how to use cross products to solve the proportion $1/3 = n/9$

$3 \times n = 1 \times 9$, or $3n = 9$. Divide each side by 3 to isolate the variable on one side. This leaves $n = 3$. The missing number in the proportion is 3: $1/3 = 3/9$. Say "one is to three as three is to nine."

TEST EXAMPLE

1 Which number correctly completes the proportion? $2/3 = 14/n$
- Ⓐ 19
- Ⓑ 21
- Ⓒ 23
- Ⓓ 28

THINK ABOUT THE ANSWER

The answer is option B. Using cross products, $2 \times n = 3 \times 14$, or $2n = 42$. Divide each side by 2 to isolate the variable on one side. This leaves $n = 21$. The missing number in the proportion is 21: $2/3 = 14/21$.

NOW YOU TRY IT

2 Rewrite the ratios $n:6$ and $25:30$ as a proportion and solve for the missing number.
- Ⓕ 150
- Ⓖ 30
- Ⓗ 5
- Ⓙ 1

Check your answer on page 111.

Not the Same
Be careful with ratios and proportions. A 2:1 ratio is not the same as a 1:2 ratio.

Practice Test Introduction

The rest of this book is a practice test. It's like the standardized test you will have to take for real. On this practice test, you'll have a chance to use all the skills you've gained by working through the lessons in this book.

The test is divided into the same sections as the earlier parts of the book. There's a test on reading, writing, language, and math. The questions in each test are similar to the ones you've been practicing. Use the answer sheets on the next two pages for answering each test. The answer sheet is divided up in the same way as the practice test itself, with four sections.

Here are some tips to keep in mind as you take the practice tests.

- Don't worry if you're a little nervous. In fact, being a little nervous can sometimes help you to do your best.
- Remember the Testwise suggestions you read at the bottom of each practice page. They can help you on the practice test, just like they can help you on the real thing.
- Make sure you understand all the directions before you start a test. Ask an adult if you have any questions about the directions.
- Unlike a real standardized test, there's no time limit on this practice test. However, try to work as quickly as you can. Working quickly will give you practice in managing your time.
- If you don't know an answer, you can guess at it or skip it to come back to later.
- Try to complete each section of the test, such as the reading test or the math test, at one time. You'll probably want to take a break between tests.
- After finishing each test, check yourself. Use the answer key to each test. You'll find the practice test answers at the very back of the book starting on page 109.

Student Information Sheet

Complete this student information sheet. It is similar to ones found on tests. Be sure to fill in the correct bubble for each letter of your name.

STUDENT'S NAME — LAST, FIRST, MI (bubbles A–Z for each letter column)

SCHOOL

TEACHER

FEMALE ○   MALE ○

BIRTHDATE

MONTH	DAY	YEAR
JAN ○	0	0 0
FEB ○	1	1 1
MAR ○	2	2 2
APR ○	3	3 3
MAY ○	4	4 4
JUN ○	5	5 5
JUL ○	6	6 6
AUG ○	7	7 7
SEP ○	8	8 8
OCT ○	9	9 9
NOV ○		
DEC ○		

GRADE

④ ⑤ ⑥ ⑦ ⑧

Practice Test Answer Sheet

READING

1. Ⓐ Ⓑ Ⓒ Ⓓ
2. Ⓕ Ⓖ Ⓗ Ⓙ
3. Written answer
4. Ⓕ Ⓖ Ⓗ Ⓙ
5. Written answer
6. Ⓕ Ⓖ Ⓗ Ⓙ
7. Ⓐ Ⓑ Ⓒ Ⓓ
8. Written answer
9. Ⓐ Ⓑ Ⓒ Ⓓ
10. Ⓕ Ⓖ Ⓗ Ⓙ
11. Ⓐ Ⓑ Ⓒ Ⓓ
12. Written answer
13. Ⓐ Ⓑ Ⓒ Ⓓ
14. Ⓕ Ⓖ Ⓗ Ⓙ
15. Ⓐ Ⓑ Ⓒ Ⓓ
16. Ⓕ Ⓖ Ⓗ Ⓙ
17. Written answer
18. Ⓕ Ⓖ Ⓗ Ⓙ
19. Ⓐ Ⓑ Ⓒ Ⓓ
20. Written answer
21. Ⓐ Ⓑ Ⓒ Ⓓ
22. Ⓕ Ⓖ Ⓗ Ⓙ
23. Written answer
24. Ⓕ Ⓖ Ⓗ Ⓙ
25. Ⓐ Ⓑ Ⓒ Ⓓ
26. Ⓕ Ⓖ Ⓗ Ⓙ
27. Ⓐ Ⓑ Ⓒ Ⓓ
28. Written answer
29. Ⓐ Ⓑ Ⓒ Ⓓ
30. Ⓕ Ⓖ Ⓗ Ⓙ

LANGUAGE

31. Ⓐ Ⓑ Ⓒ Ⓓ
32. Ⓕ Ⓖ Ⓗ Ⓙ
33. Ⓐ Ⓑ Ⓒ Ⓓ
34. Written answer
35. Ⓐ Ⓑ Ⓒ Ⓓ
36. Ⓕ Ⓖ Ⓗ Ⓙ
37. Ⓐ Ⓑ Ⓒ Ⓓ
38. Ⓕ Ⓖ Ⓗ Ⓙ
39. Ⓐ Ⓑ Ⓒ Ⓓ
40. Ⓕ Ⓖ Ⓗ Ⓙ
41. Ⓐ Ⓑ Ⓒ Ⓓ
42. Ⓕ Ⓖ Ⓗ Ⓙ
43. Ⓐ Ⓑ Ⓒ Ⓓ
44. Ⓕ Ⓖ Ⓗ Ⓙ
45. Ⓐ Ⓑ Ⓒ Ⓓ
46. Ⓕ Ⓖ Ⓗ Ⓙ
47. Ⓐ Ⓑ Ⓒ Ⓓ
48. Ⓕ Ⓖ Ⓗ Ⓙ
49. Ⓐ Ⓑ Ⓒ Ⓓ
50. Ⓕ Ⓖ Ⓗ Ⓙ
51. Ⓐ Ⓑ Ⓒ Ⓓ
52. Ⓕ Ⓖ Ⓗ Ⓙ
53. Written answer
54. Written answer
55. Ⓐ Ⓑ Ⓒ Ⓓ
56. Ⓕ Ⓖ Ⓗ Ⓙ
57. Ⓐ Ⓑ Ⓒ Ⓓ
58. Ⓕ Ⓖ Ⓗ Ⓙ
59. Ⓐ Ⓑ Ⓒ Ⓓ
60. Written answer

MATH

61. Ⓐ Ⓑ Ⓒ Ⓓ
62. Ⓕ Ⓖ Ⓗ Ⓙ
63. Ⓐ Ⓑ Ⓒ Ⓓ
64. Ⓕ Ⓖ Ⓗ Ⓙ
65. Ⓐ Ⓑ Ⓒ Ⓓ
66. Ⓕ Ⓖ Ⓗ Ⓙ
67. Ⓐ Ⓑ Ⓒ Ⓓ
68. Ⓕ Ⓖ Ⓗ Ⓙ
69. Ⓐ Ⓑ Ⓒ Ⓓ
70. Ⓕ Ⓖ Ⓗ Ⓙ
71. Ⓐ Ⓑ Ⓒ Ⓓ
72. Ⓕ Ⓖ Ⓗ Ⓙ
73. Ⓐ Ⓑ Ⓒ Ⓓ
74. Ⓕ Ⓖ Ⓗ Ⓙ
75. Ⓐ Ⓑ Ⓒ Ⓓ
76. Ⓕ Ⓖ Ⓗ Ⓙ
77. Ⓐ Ⓑ Ⓒ Ⓓ
78. Ⓕ Ⓖ Ⓗ Ⓙ
79. Ⓐ Ⓑ Ⓒ Ⓓ
80. Ⓕ Ⓖ Ⓗ Ⓙ
81. Ⓐ Ⓑ Ⓒ Ⓓ
82. Ⓕ Ⓖ Ⓗ Ⓙ
83. Ⓐ Ⓑ Ⓒ Ⓓ
84. Ⓕ Ⓖ Ⓗ Ⓙ
85. Ⓐ Ⓑ Ⓒ Ⓓ
86. Ⓕ Ⓖ Ⓗ Ⓙ
87. Ⓐ Ⓑ Ⓒ Ⓓ
88. Ⓕ Ⓖ Ⓗ Ⓙ
89. Ⓐ Ⓑ Ⓒ Ⓓ
90. Ⓕ Ⓖ Ⓗ Ⓙ
91. Ⓐ Ⓑ Ⓒ Ⓓ
92. Ⓕ Ⓖ Ⓗ Ⓙ
93. Ⓐ Ⓑ Ⓒ Ⓓ
94. Ⓕ Ⓖ Ⓗ Ⓙ
95. Ⓐ Ⓑ Ⓒ Ⓓ
96. Ⓕ Ⓖ Ⓗ Ⓙ
97. Ⓐ Ⓑ Ⓒ Ⓓ
98. Ⓕ Ⓖ Ⓗ Ⓙ
99. Ⓐ Ⓑ Ⓒ Ⓓ
100. Ⓕ Ⓖ Ⓗ Ⓙ
101. Ⓐ Ⓑ Ⓒ Ⓓ

PRACTICE TEST: READING

Read the passage about one of the world's great rivers. Then answer questions 1 through 15.

The Father of Waters

From its source at Lake Itasca, Minnesota, to its mouth southeast of New Orleans, America's mightiest river cuts a broad path through the nation's heartland. However, the path it has cut through the nation's imagination and history may be even broader. The river is the Mississippi. Its name, from two Alogonkin words, could not be more appropriate. These Native Americans called the river "Father of Waters."

Along its length of about 2,350 miles (3,780 kilometers), the Mississippi can be divided into four different stages. Looking at the river at these four different stages, it would be difficult to tell it was the same river. From its source to St. Paul, the highest navigable point, the Mississippi looks more like a stream, clear and calm. Past St. Paul, the widening and deepening upper Mississippi flows past high limestone cliffs. Just north of St. Louis, the river is joined by one of its great tributaries. The rushing waters of the Missouri load the river with sand and other sediments. About 200 miles (382 kilometers) down-river, another great American river, the Ohio, joins the Mississippi. Here, the river reaches it full power and grandeur. At times a mile-and-a-half wide, the Mississippi has become the mighty highway of many, including Tom Sawyer and Huck Finn.

From earliest times, the Mississippi has been a thoroughfare. Before the arrival of European explorers, Native Americans used the river for both transportation and food. In the 1500s, Spanish explorers like DeSoto and Frenchmen like La Salle explored the river. Moreover, each hoped to claim it for his own king. In 1803, the Mississippi and all the land it drained passed to U.S. control.

Beginning with the Louisiana Purchase, the river began to work its way into America's consciousness. Lewis and Clark traveled on it in their expedition across the west. Zebulon Pike searched for its source. A growing trade, comprised of many different products and carried on flatboats, rafts, and keelboats, filled the river. By mid-century, the Mississippi was one of the most important rivers in the world. Its legendary steamboats, "palaces on paddle wheels," carried passengers, cotton, and other cargo.

The river and its traffic fired the dreams of many people, including a young boy growing up in the Missouri river town of Hannibal. Young Sam Clemens watched the boats come and go on the river, eventually fulfilling his dream of working on the river. Hearing the calls of river men helped him choose a new name, by which he became world-famous. Mark Twain means the river was just deep enough for a steamboat to pass. Few people have done more to immortalize the Mississippi River.

Today, the Mississippi carries immense amounts of cargo. Boats as long as 1,500 feet (457 meters) carry cargoes like oil, coal, iron and steel, sand, gravel, chemicals, and even the giant booster engines that lift rockets into space.

1 Few people have done more to <u>immortalize</u> the Mississippi River. Which answer is a synonym with *immortalize*?

- Ⓐ make famous forever
- Ⓑ write stories about
- Ⓒ praise
- Ⓓ name

2 Which sentence from the selection uses figurative language?

- Ⓕ Lewis and Clark traveled on it in their expedition across the west.
- Ⓖ However, the path it has cut through the nation's imagination and history may be even broader.
- Ⓗ Looking at the river at these four different stages, it would be difficult to tell it was the same river.
- Ⓙ Before the arrival of European explorers, Native Americans used the river for both transportation and food.

3 Write a one-sentence summary of the second paragraph of the selection.

_____

_____

4 What is the best category name for the following information from the text?
Lewis and Clark, Zebulon Pike, growing trade, great steamboats

- Ⓕ ways the Mississippi became known to Americans
- Ⓖ cargoes carried on the river
- Ⓗ the Louisiana Purchase
- Ⓙ famous explorers

5 Write a sentence that explains how the ways early Native Americans and modern Americans use the Mississippi River are similar.

_____

_____

Practice Test: Reading

6 Which sentence is an opinion?
- Ⓕ From earliest times, the Mississippi has been a thoroughfare.
- Ⓖ Its name, from two Alogonkin words, could not be more appropriate.
- Ⓗ A growing trade, comprised of many different products and carried on flatboats, rafts, and keelboats, filled the river.
- Ⓙ Boats as long as 1,500 feet (457 meters) carry cargoes like oil, coal, iron and steel, sand, gravel, chemicals, and even the giant booster engines that lift rockets into space.

7 Which passage contains a transitional word?
- Ⓐ These Native Americans called the river "Father of Waters."
- Ⓑ In 1803, the Mississippi and all the land it drained passed to U.S. control.
- Ⓒ However, the path it has cut through the nation's imagination may be even broader.
- Ⓓ Looking at the river at these three different stages, it would be difficult to tell it was the same river.

8 Write two sentences to explain how the explorers DeSoto and La Salle were similar and how they were different.

_____

_____

_____

9 Which persuasive technique does the author use to convince readers that the Mississippi is an important part of American history and culture?
- Ⓐ repeating key points
- Ⓑ using colorful language
- Ⓒ anticipating and answering opposing viewpoints
- Ⓓ all of the above

10 Choose the word or words that mean the same thing as the underlined word.
From its source to St. Paul, the highest <u>navigable</u> point, the Mississippi looks more like a stream, clear and calm.
- Ⓕ beautiful
- Ⓖ reportable
- Ⓗ dangerous
- Ⓙ passable by large ships

GO →

11 Into what three categories could you classify the information about the river in this selection?
- Ⓐ nature, history, and culture
- Ⓑ dreams, reality, and history
- Ⓒ flatboats, keelboats, and steamboats
- Ⓓ Native Americans, French, and Spanish

12 Write a two-sentence summary of the fifth paragraph of the selection.

_____

_____

_____

13 Which sentence from the selection uses figurative language?
- Ⓐ Today, the Mississippi carries immense amounts of cargo.
- Ⓑ By mid-century, the Mississippi was one of the most important rivers in the world.
- Ⓒ At times a mile-and-a-half wide, the Mississippi has become the mighty highway of many, including Tom Sawyer and Huck Finn.
- Ⓓ Young Sam Clemens watched the boats come and go on the river, eventually fulfilling his dream of working on the river.

14 Which passage contains a transitional word?
- Ⓕ Here, the river reaches it full power and grandeur.
- Ⓖ Just north of St. Louis, the river is joined by one of its great tributaries.
- Ⓗ These Native Americans called the river "Father of Waters."
- Ⓙ Looking at the river at these four different stages, it would be difficult to tell it was the same river.

15 All of the following statements are facts EXCEPT—
- Ⓐ Lewis and Clark traveled on the river in their expedition across the west.
- Ⓑ Mark Twain means the river was just deep enough for a steamboat to pass.
- Ⓒ The rushing waters of the Missouri load the river with sand and other sediments.
- Ⓓ However, the path it has cut through the nation's imagination and history may be even broader.

Practice Test: Reading

Read the story, a tale from the Mississippi riverboat days. Then answer questions 16 through 25.

An old, gray-haired woman had decided to travel down the river from her home in Kentucky to visit relatives in New Orleans. She was taking with her several large barrels of home-made lard from her farm. These she planned to sell at the big New Orleans market.

As she waited on the dock to board the great white riverboat, she looked worried. The woman had never traveled on a riverboat before. Her friends had told her terrible stories about the dangers of traveling by riverboat. The boats could hit snags or shoals in the water, they could collide with other boats, or they could catch fire. But one danger frightened her more than any other. Riverboat captains sometimes challenged each other to races. To reach top speed—and even go beyond what was safe—the great boats built up more and more pressure in their steam boilers. Every now and then, the pressure would become too great. The boilers would burst, causing catastrophic explosions that killed many people.

As she boarded the boat, the woman met the captain. She said earnestly, "Captain, promise me you won't race."

The captain replied, "Madam, I never, ever race. Or almost never. I promise I will do nothing to imperil you."

"Thank you, Captain," she answered. "I feel much safer."

The great boat steamed serenely down the river for several days, like a great white swan. One afternoon, however, another boat came up beside it. The crew members on each boat began railing at each other. The insults flew from boat to boat until the firemen who fed the boilers began to throw more and more wood into the fiery furnace.

The Kentucky woman began to wring her hands. "Oh my," she wailed, "this is a race!" She watched the rival boat slowly inch ahead. Her eyes grew narrow and her breaths short. Suddenly, she darted up the stairs and burst into the cabin.

"Captain!" she shouted. "You can forget about your promise. I'm from Kentucky, where horse racing is king. I can't stand to lose a race!"

The captain smiled and answered, "Madam, I'm afraid we're doing the best we can." Then he continued, "The other boat is putting oil in her boilers along with the wood. It makes the wood burn hotter. We can't keep up because we don't have any oil."

The woman gazed for a few moments at the other boat. It was pulling ahead slowly but surely, using the extra power from the oil in her boilers.

"Captain, where is my lard?" she asked.

"Why, it's safe in the cargo hold."

"Bring it up this minute and throw it into the boilers!" she commanded. "We'll beat that old pile of scrap if it's the last thing I do!"

The captain gave the order, and up came the lard. The boat trembled and strained. Thick black smoke poured out of the smokestacks. The great paddle wheel turned faster and faster. Then, with the old woman standing on the deck, the boat began to pull ahead of the other boat. The Kentucky woman laughed and waved good-bye to their defeated rival.

16 Choose the word or words that mean the same thing as the underlined word.
I promise I will do nothing to imperil you.
- Ⓕ upset
- Ⓖ anger
- Ⓗ frighten
- Ⓙ endanger

17 Write a three-sentence summary of the story.

_____

_____

_____

_____

_____

18 Which sentence from the selection uses figurative language?
- Ⓕ The crew members on each boat began railing at each other.
- Ⓖ The other boat is putting oil in her boilers along with the wood.
- Ⓗ The great boat steamed serenely down the river for several days, like a great white swan.
- Ⓙ It was pulling ahead slowly but surely, using the extra power from the oil in her boilers.

19 Which sentence from the selection contains a transitional word?
- Ⓐ I'm from Kentucky, where horse racing is king.
- Ⓑ One afternoon, however, another boat came up beside it.
- Ⓒ Riverboat captains sometimes challenged each other to races.
- Ⓓ It was pulling ahead slowly but surely, using the extra power from the oil in her boilers.

20 Look at the word below. Write a word with the same denotation, but a negative connotation. Then write a word with the same denotation, but a positive connotation.

Word	Negative Connotation	Positive Connotation
old	_____	_____

GO →

Practice Test: Reading

21 Imagine you are the author of this story. What title would you give it to give your readers a little help in predicting the outcome of the story?
- Ⓐ On the River
- Ⓑ The Old Woman
- Ⓒ A Change of Heart
- Ⓓ Horse Racing Is a Lot Like Boat Racing

22 Which of the following sentences from the story tells relevant information about why the old woman changed her mind about racing?
- Ⓕ An old, gray-haired woman had decided to travel down the river from her home in Kentucky to visit relatives in New Orleans.
- Ⓖ Her friends had told her terrible stories about the dangers of traveling by riverboat.
- Ⓗ The boilers would burst, causing catastrophic explosions that killed many people.
- Ⓙ She was taking with her several large barrels of home-made lard from her farm.

23 Describe the setting of the story.

_____

_____

_____

24 Choose the word that means the same thing as the underlined word.
The great boat steamed <u>serenely</u> down the river for several days, like a great white swan.
- Ⓕ calmly
- Ⓖ slowly
- Ⓗ quickly
- Ⓙ hurriedly

25 From whose point of view is the story told?
- Ⓐ an old woman
- Ⓑ the riverboat captain
- Ⓒ a third person involved in the story
- Ⓓ a third person not involved in the story

Read the table. Then answer questions 26 through 28.

Population Data on Important Mississippi River Cities

City	Population 2000	Change 1990–2000
Minneapolis	382,618	3.9%
St. Paul	287,151	5.5%
St. Louis	348,189	-12.2%
Memphis	650,100	6.5%
Baton Rouge	227,818	3.8%
New Orleans	484,674	-2.5%

26 Which cities lost population from 1990 to 2000?
- Ⓕ St. Louis and Memphis
- Ⓖ St. Louis and St. Paul
- Ⓗ St. Paul and New Orleans
- Ⓙ New Orleans and St. Louis

27 Which city grew the fastest from 1990 to 2000?
- Ⓐ St. Paul
- Ⓑ St. Louis
- Ⓒ Memphis
- Ⓓ Baton Rouge

28 Which city do you expect to have a larger population in the year 2010, Minneapolis or St. Louis? Why?

_____

_____

Read the dictionary entry. Then answer questions 29 and 30.

al·lu·vi·um (ə-lōō' vē-əm) *n.* Sediment deposited by moving water, as in a river bed, flood plain, or delta. Also called *alluvion*. [Medieval Latin, flood, from neuter of Latin *alluvius*, alluvial, from *alluere*, to wash against. See ALLUVION.]

29 Which word rhymes with the vowel in the second syllable of *alluvium*?
- Ⓐ bug
- Ⓑ blue
- Ⓒ boat
- Ⓓ howl

30 What part of speech is *alluvium*?
- Ⓕ verb
- Ⓖ noun
- Ⓗ adverb
- Ⓙ Baton adjective

Practice Test: Writing

Writing Prompt
Think about a hobby or special interest of yours. Maybe it's playing a sport, building things, playing an instrument, hunting or fishing, or anything you enjoy that takes some special skills. Write an essay explaining the skills needed for your hobby or special interest. How did you develop them?

Your essay will be scored according to this checklist. You can use this checklist to write an essay that will earn a good score. Write a first draft, then check it against the checklist. Make improvements. Then write your final draft.

You will earn your best score if:

☐ My essay has a beginning, a middle, and an end.

☐ My essay has main ideas supported by details.

☐ The reader will understand what I wrote about.

☐ I have spelled everything right.

☐ My sentences are varied and lively.

☐ The antecedents of my pronouns are clear and in agreement with the pronouns.

☐ My sentences and proper names start with capital letters.

☐ My sentences end with a period, a question mark, or an exclamation mark.

☐ All punctuations marks are used correctly.

GO →

Plan Your Writing

Use these pages to plan your writing. The more planning you do now, the less revising you will have to do later. You might find this graphic organizer helpful.

Main Idea

Supporting Details

Write Your First Draft

Use all the skills you have learned to write a first draft. Use an extra sheet of paper if necessary.

_____

_____

_____

_____

_____

_____

_____

Practice Test: Writing

Write Your Final Draft

Now it's time to write your final draft. Use an extra sheet of paper if necessary. Use the writer's checklist on page 90 to make sure that you will achieve the best possible score. Carefully proofread your work when you are done.

Practice Test: Writing

_____
_____
_____
_____
_____
_____
_____
_____
_____
_____

Give Yourself a Score

Go back to the scoring rubric on page 31. Use the rubric to score your work. Give yourself a score from 4 to 0 for each category. Then ask someone else to score your writing and compare the scores.

How I Scored It

Content and Ideas	Organization	Sentence Structure and Clarity	Spelling, Punctuation, Usage, and Grammar
_____	_____	_____	_____

How Someone Else Scored It

Content and Ideas	Organization	Sentence Structure and Clarity	Spelling, Punctuation, Usage, and Grammar
_____	_____	_____	_____

Practice Test: Language

31 Choose the option with the correct spelling to complete the sentence.

Mr. Singh had _____ to wash his car today, but it started to rain.

- Ⓐ pland
- Ⓑ planed
- Ⓒ plannd
- Ⓓ planned

32 Which sentence contains an appositive?

- Ⓕ Mr. Zippy, the clown from TV, passed out balloons during the parade.
- Ⓖ Grandpa lost his glasses, which he needs to do the crossword.
- Ⓗ Pick up your dirty clothes, and put them in the hamper.
- Ⓙ The boy, whose left arm is in a cast, asked for help.

33 Which sentence does NOT correctly use an infinitive?

- Ⓐ Would you like to watch a movie?
- Ⓑ Jon went to Minneapolis last winter.
- Ⓒ To lock the car is always a good idea.
- Ⓓ Does Maria want to go to summer school?

34 Write an adverb that completes the sentence.

As we watched in fascination, the geese honked and _____ rose into the sky.

35 Choose the sentence that uses correct punctuation and capitalization.

- Ⓐ Call your grandmother at the Office to ask her about the Boston marathon.
- Ⓑ Call your Grandmother at the office to ask her about the Boston Marathon?
- Ⓒ Call your grandmother at the office to ask her about the Boston Marathon.
- Ⓓ call your Grandmother at the office to ask her about the Boston marathon.

Practice Test: Language

36 Choose the option with the correct spelling to complete the sentence.
Mrs. Jackson _____ home as the wind picked up and the sprinkles began to fall.
- Ⓕ huried
- Ⓖ hurried
- Ⓗ hurryed
- Ⓙ hurreyed

37 Which of the following is NOT an interrogative sentence?
- Ⓐ When I arrive, I'll tell you the whole story
- Ⓑ Where did you get your laptop
- Ⓒ Don't you just want to scream
- Ⓓ Is Jacob in that class

38 Which sentence correctly uses colons or semicolons?
- Ⓕ Listen, Karim to what the coach is saying.
- Ⓖ Don't move that chair; and don't move the table either!
- Ⓗ Without a care in the world I sprinted through the woods.
- Ⓙ We heard the band; soon after, the marchers came into view.

39 Which sentence uses subordination to link more important and less important ideas?
- Ⓐ We want to see the game because it's going to be a great one.
- Ⓑ Pets are fun, but a lot of people can't have them because of allergies.
- Ⓒ Lime, which is an alkali, can restore fields that have been fertilized a lot.
- Ⓓ Jack put paper bags over the young plants so they wouldn't freeze overnight.

40 Which of the following is NOT an interrogative sentence and should NOT end with a question mark?
- Ⓕ When does the movie start?
- Ⓖ Where is that small paint brush?
- Ⓗ What on earth are you chattering about?
- Ⓙ What he wants for his birthday is a secret?

41 Which sentence does NOT contain an adjective?
- Ⓐ The forest is slowly turning green as the temperatures rise.
- Ⓑ Fortunately, I made the bus with seconds to spare.
- Ⓒ We don't like cars that are too big.
- Ⓓ For Marcus, it's a personal thing.

42 Choose the option with the correct spelling to complete the sentence.
After picking for two hours, we had several buckets full of juicy ripe _____ .
- Ⓕ strawberreys
- Ⓖ strawberries
- Ⓗ strawberrys
- Ⓙ strawberry

43 Which sentence is correct?
- Ⓐ I've never seen one of her movies (that wasn't great).
- Ⓑ Have you decided if you're going [I definitely am!] to the game?
- Ⓒ The first line is, "The curfew tolls [rings] the knell of passing day."
- Ⓓ Rosa picked the flowers from the garden the one on the south side of the house.

44 Which sentence does NOT use parallel construction correctly?
- Ⓕ Ice cream is good, cake is tasty, and I like fruit pies, too.
- Ⓖ We can't wait to go to the concert and listen to the bands.
- Ⓗ Thea enjoys playing volleyball and working out at the gym.
- Ⓙ The campfire crackled, the crickets chirped, and an owl hooted.

45 Choose the sentence that does NOT use hyphenation correctly.
- Ⓐ George Washington was born into a well-to-do Virginia family.
- Ⓑ Close to three-fourths of the sheep were already sheared.
- Ⓒ Don't you think Monica is a little self-centered?
- Ⓓ Jason's dad is thirty-four.

Practice Test: Language

46 Choose the answer that best completes the sentence.
When Ben and Josh come in, ask _____ to take off their shoes.
- Ⓕ it
- Ⓖ him
- Ⓗ they
- Ⓙ them

47 Look at the underlined words. Which is spelled correctly?
- Ⓐ What's your <u>strategy</u> for answering difficult questions?
- Ⓑ The candidate is about to make an important <u>statment</u>.
- Ⓒ *Gulliver's Travels* is a true classic of world <u>literture</u>.
- Ⓓ When is your parents' <u>aniversary</u>?

48 Which sentence does NOT correctly use a present or past participle?
- Ⓕ Understanding the problem at last, Jonathan smiled with satisfaction.
- Ⓖ Ms. Patterson, distracted by the flashing lights, did not see the sign.
- Ⓗ Sitting in the bathtub, I felt the ache in my back lessen.
- Ⓙ Mark and Liz decided they were hearing things.

49 Which sentence is correct?
- Ⓐ You can come in; but she can't.
- Ⓑ Look Dad, there's a squirrel on the bird feeder!
- Ⓒ Looking for his lost flashlight, Maurice searched the tent.
- Ⓓ Hats aren't allowed in class, please hang them on the pegs by the door.

50 Choose the sentence that does NOT use hyphenation correctly.
- Ⓕ Jenna's makeup for the play included an ugly-looking scar.
- Ⓖ One-half of the students received the long form of the math test.
- Ⓗ The roll call was two-thirds completed when the lights went out.
- Ⓙ Thirty-nine of the birds in the pet shop were sold over the weekend.

51 In which sentence is the gerund phrase underlined?

- Ⓐ <u>Swimming</u> in the ocean is a lot of fun.
- Ⓑ The nanny <u>is taking the children to the park</u>.
- Ⓒ Have you ever thought about <u>joining the Spanish Club</u>?
- Ⓓ The baby, <u>crying loudly</u>, sat on the doctor's examining table.

52 Choose the sentence that uses correct punctuation and capitalization.

- Ⓕ His Uncle said, "The Empire State Building is an impressive sight."
- Ⓖ His uncle said, "The Empire State Building is an impressive sight."
- Ⓗ His uncle said, "The empire state building is an impressive sight."
- Ⓙ His uncle said, "the Empire State Building is an impressive sight."

Read this paragraph. Then answer questions 53 and 54.

Many people may be surprised to learn something interesting. Salamanders are not related to reptiles. Some reptiles are lizards, snakes, and crocodiles. Salamanders are related to frogs and other amphibians. Amphibians are animals that begin life under water. They breathe with gills. Then they age. They develop lungs and become land creatures.

53 Combine the first three sentences in a way that will add variety and liveliness to the paragraph.

_____

_____

_____

54 Combine the last four sentences in a way that will add variety and liveliness to the paragraph.

_____

_____

_____

55 Which sentence correctly uses parallel construction?

- Ⓐ Does she want to come with us or stay home?
- Ⓑ The happy puppy wagged her tail and was licking my hand.
- Ⓒ To set up a computer and learning to operate it are not too difficult.
- Ⓓ Douglas and his brother don't like playing video games or to surf the Internet.

Practice Test: Language

56 Look at the underlined words. Which is spelled correctly?
- Ⓕ Are there any more seats <u>avalable</u> for the Saturday night performance?
- Ⓖ Memorial Day is for <u>rememberance</u> of people who have died in wars.
- Ⓗ It's necessary to have a ticket to enter the <u>exhibition</u>.
- Ⓙ All he does is <u>complane</u> about the cafeteria food!

57 Choose the answer that best completes the sentence.
Amanda discovered to _____ embarrassment that she was in the wrong building.
- Ⓐ she
- Ⓑ her
- Ⓒ our
- Ⓓ their

58 Look at the underlined words. Which is spelled incorrectly?
- Ⓕ The factory closed <u>permanently</u> last winter.
- Ⓖ The vote in favor of the proposal was almost <u>unanimous</u>.
- Ⓗ Margaret is <u>desperate</u> to get into the advanced math class.
- Ⓙ How much <u>witholding</u> is taken out of your paycheck each week?

59 In which sentence is the gerund phrase underlined?
- Ⓐ I would hate <u>to be late for your party</u>.
- Ⓑ Look at that monkey <u>swinging on a tire</u>!
- Ⓒ I will be <u>looking for you in front of the grocery store</u>.
- Ⓓ <u>Watching the lambs</u> made me want to live on a farm.

60 Write a sentence that uses an adverb. Circle the adverb.

_____

_____

_____

100

Advantage Test Prep Grade 8 © 2005 Creative Teaching Press

Practice Test: Mathematics

61. Which of the following is a reasonable estimation of the answer to this multiplication problem: 746 x 1/3?
- Ⓐ 25
- Ⓑ 74
- Ⓒ 150
- Ⓓ 250

62. Jacquie makes paper flowers to sell at a church holiday sale. She needs to make 280 flowers. If she can make four flowers an hour, and can spend ten hours a week making them, how many weeks will she need to make all her flowers?
- Ⓕ 4
- Ⓖ 7
- Ⓗ 10
- Ⓙ 28

63. Which group of numbers is written in order from least to greatest?
- Ⓐ 445,485; 544,584; 554,845
- Ⓑ 19; 32; -40
- Ⓒ 1/2; 1/4; 1/3
- Ⓓ -6; 12; -21

64. 27.196 ÷ 1.529 = _____
- Ⓕ 0.17787
- Ⓖ 1.7787
- Ⓗ 17.787
- Ⓙ 177.87

65. The least common multiple of 6, 10, and 12 is _____.
- Ⓐ 18
- Ⓑ 24
- Ⓒ 30
- Ⓓ 60

Practice Test: Mathematics

66 The rainfall during one rainy five-day period in spring was 1.13, 0.21, 0.74, 0.02, and 0.56 inches. What was the range of the rainfall?
- Ⓕ 2.66 inches
- Ⓖ 1.11 inches
- Ⓗ 0.56 inches
- Ⓙ 0.53 inches

67 Ms. Fukuzawa's car gets 24 miles per gallon. The car's gas tank holds 14.7 gallons of gasoline. How far can she expect to drive on a full tank of gas?
- Ⓐ 3,528 miles
- Ⓑ 352.8 miles
- Ⓒ 240 miles
- Ⓓ 147 miles

68 Which of the following is a reasonable estimate of the answer to this division problem?
595 ÷ 38.2 = _____
- Ⓕ 15
- Ⓖ 20
- Ⓗ 50
- Ⓙ 150

69 A dart board is divided into 32 equal-sized sections, numbered 1 to 32. If you threw two darts without aiming, what are the chances you would get two darts in section 32 in two tosses?
- Ⓐ 1/32
- Ⓑ 2/32
- Ⓒ 2/1024
- Ⓓ 1/1024

70 Rewrite the ratios 4/*n* and 64:80 as a proportion and solve for the missing number.
- Ⓕ 9
- Ⓖ 8
- Ⓗ 5
- Ⓙ 4

71 What is the length of side *a* in this triangle?

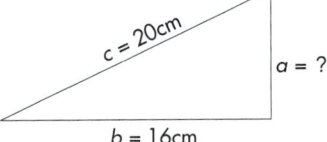

- Ⓐ 8 cm
- Ⓑ 10 cm
- Ⓒ 12 cm
- Ⓓ 14 cm

72 What is the volume of this solid?

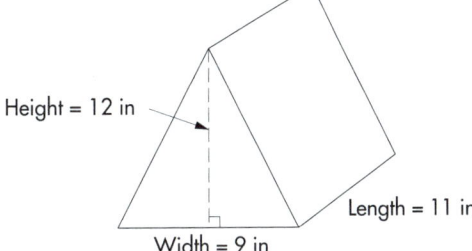

- Ⓕ 132 in^3
- Ⓖ 594 in^3
- Ⓗ 896 in^3
- Ⓙ 1,188 in^3

73 Which number correctly completes the proportion?

7/11 = 35/n

- Ⓐ 55
- Ⓑ 52
- Ⓒ 49
- Ⓓ 45

74 Jason wants to buy a new BMX bike. The bike's price is $269.95. The sales tax in his state is 6 1/2%. How much will the total cost for the new bike be?

- Ⓕ $17.55
- Ⓖ $276.45
- Ⓗ $287.50
- Ⓙ $294.91

75 2.9×10^{-5} = _____

- Ⓐ 0.00029
- Ⓑ 0.000029
- Ⓒ 0.0000029
- Ⓓ 0.00000029

Practice Test: Mathematics

76 17 × (-5) = _____
- Ⓕ 12
- Ⓖ -12
- Ⓗ 85
- Ⓙ -85

77 Which of the following pairs does NOT represent a ratio of 7:2?
- Ⓐ 14:4
- Ⓑ 28:8
- Ⓒ 34:10
- Ⓓ 42:12

78 Which graph shows the equation $x - 1 = y$?

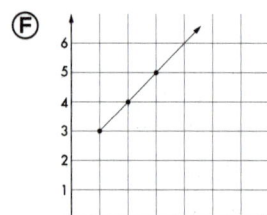 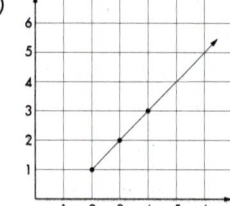 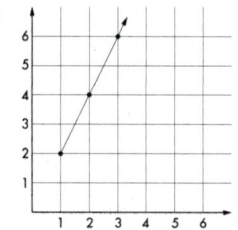 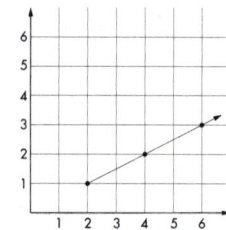

79 On a map of the Chicago area, the scale is 1 inch = 4 1/2 miles. How far is it from the Sears Tower downtown to Northwestern University if the two places are 2 2/3 inches apart on the map?
- Ⓐ 2 2/3 miles
- Ⓑ 6 1/2 miles
- Ⓒ 12 miles
- Ⓓ 18 miles

80 Felicia has 5 pennies in her pocket. The dates on the pennies are 2004, 2002, 2000, 1997, and 1991. What is the probability that she will pull out the two newest pennies on consecutive tries, if she puts the first penny back into her pocket?
- Ⓕ 2/5
- Ⓖ 1/20
- Ⓗ 1/25
- Ⓙ 1/50

81 -65 x (-22) = _____
- Ⓐ -1430
- Ⓑ 1430
- Ⓒ 87
- Ⓓ -87

82 If this shape is flipped across line GH, what will it look like?

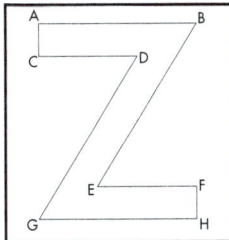

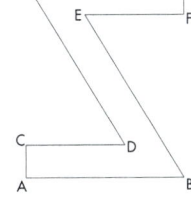 Ⓕ

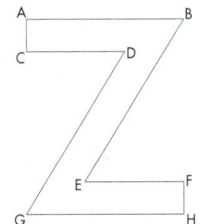 Ⓖ

Ⓗ

83 1.64 ÷ 0.52 = _____
- Ⓐ 315
- Ⓑ 31.5
- Ⓒ 3.15
- Ⓓ .315

84 What is the ratio of 24:56?
- Ⓕ 3:6
- Ⓖ 3:7
- Ⓗ 4:7
- Ⓙ 1:2

85 Which pair of figures is NOT congruent?

86 What is the volume of this solid?
- Ⓕ 250 in^3
- Ⓖ 480 in^3
- Ⓗ 500 in^3
- Ⓙ 840 in^3

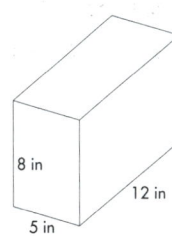

GO

Practice Test: Mathematics

87 $5.9 \times 10^6 - 4.8 \times 10^4 =$ _____
- Ⓐ 5.852×10^6
- Ⓑ 5.852×10^4
- Ⓒ 585.2×10^6
- Ⓓ 585.2×10^4

88 Which pair of values solves the equation $2x \div y = 3$?
- Ⓕ 2, 3
- Ⓖ 3, 2
- Ⓗ 4, 2
- Ⓙ 2, 4

89 $8.1 \times 10^{-7} =$ _____
- Ⓐ 0.0000000081
- Ⓒ 0.00000081
- Ⓑ 0.000000081
- Ⓓ 0.0000081

90 $3/4 + 3/5 =$ _____
- Ⓕ 1 1/5
- Ⓗ 1 4/5
- Ⓖ 27/20
- Ⓙ 1 7/20

91 What is the value of y in this equation if x = 4?
$x \div 2 = y - 1$
- Ⓐ 3
- Ⓒ 5
- Ⓑ 4
- Ⓓ 6

92 Shawna is the leading rebounder on her basketball team. During the 12-game season, she averaged 6.5 rebounds a game. How many rebounds did she snare during the entire season?
- Ⓕ 12
- Ⓗ 78
- Ⓖ 65
- Ⓙ 87

93 What is the value of the expression $6n - (n + 3)$ if $n = 5$?
- Ⓐ 9
- Ⓒ 28
- Ⓑ 22
- Ⓓ 32

94 If this shape is turned on point B 180° clockwise, what will it look like?

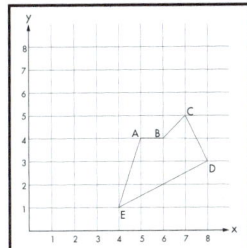

Ⓕ 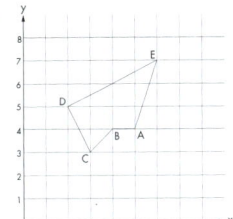   Ⓖ 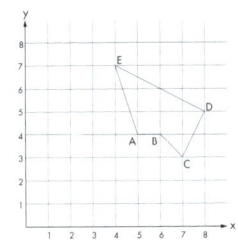   Ⓗ 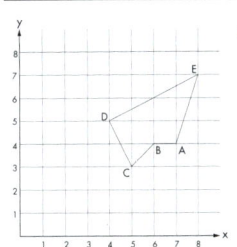   Ⓙ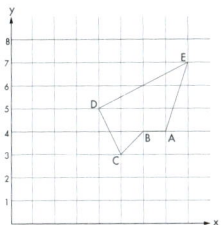

95 Look at the histogram. Then answer the question.

How many more students were born in the highest month than were born in the lowest month?

Ⓐ 12
Ⓑ 35
Ⓒ 32
Ⓓ 49

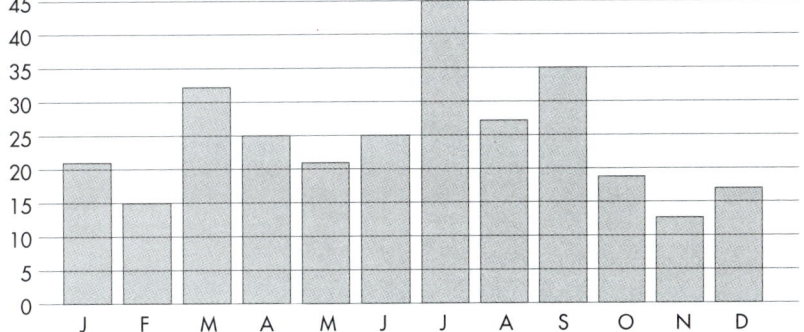

96 $2.7 \times 10^{-8} - 6.8 \times 10^{-5} =$ _____

Ⓕ 2.6932×10^{-8}
Ⓖ 2.6932×10^{-5}
Ⓗ 2.6932×10^{8}
Ⓙ $2,693.2 \times 10^{-5}$

Practice Test: Mathematics

97 If this shape is turned on point B 90° counter-clockwise, what will it look like?

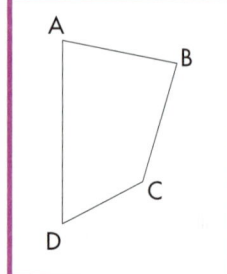 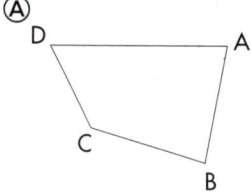 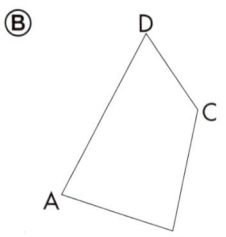 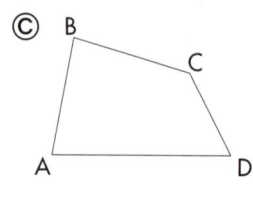

98 What is the value of the expression $4n \div (n - 2)$ if $n = 4$?
- Ⓕ 4
- Ⓖ 8
- Ⓗ 16
- Ⓙ 32

99 Which equation does the graph show?
- Ⓐ $x = y \div 2$
- Ⓑ $2x = y$
- Ⓒ $x = y + 1$
- Ⓓ $x \div 2 = y$

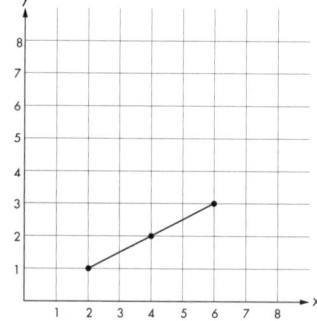

100 Kayla is going to buy a CD player. Its regular price is $79.95. For a short time, it is available for $63.96. How much of a discount will she receive?
- Ⓕ 20%
- Ⓖ 15%
- Ⓗ 10%
- Ⓙ 5%

101 48 is NOT the least common denominator of _____ .
- Ⓐ 6, 12, and 16
- Ⓑ 6, 8, and 12
- Ⓒ 6, 8, and 16
- Ⓓ 12 and 16

Answer Key

Reading

Page 8
Option F is the answer. From the context, it is evident that the word *bounty* means something good given by the river, because the Shang people depended on it. The other options, while all good things, do not communicate the meaning of something that is given.

Page 9
Option F is the answer. The bones do not literally "speak" to us. What the author means is that, through the bones, we can learn about Shang society, as if members of this long-dead civilization could "speak" and tell us about their lives.

Page 10
You could have written something like this: In order to communicate with their gods about important decisions, Shang priests scratched messages on bones and inserted hot metal rods into them. They then interpreted the pattern of cracks that appeared on the oracle bones as answers from the gods. This summary explains what oracle bones were, how they were used, and what significance they held for the Shang.

Page 11
Option G is the answer. It makes the best name because the information describes why many early peoples settled near rivers, not just the Shang (option F). Option H is not correct because this name is too broad for the specific information about river settlement. Option J is not correct because the information is not about only the Shang.

Page 12
A correct answer could have made these points: bones were used only for oracle purposes, while bronzes had other uses as well; bones brought about the first Chinese writing, while bronzes signaled a different kind of cultural and scientific advance; bones were used only by priests, while many kinds of people used bronzes.

Page 14
Words with a negative connotation include *skinny, frail, scrawny, gaunt, spindly,* or *bony*. Words with a positive connotation include *slim, lean, slender,* or *svelte*.

Page 15
The best answer is option H. It gives the reader a clue about what might happen, but does not give the story away. Option F is too obvious and gives the ending away. Options G and J are no help in predicting the outcome.

Page 16
The correct answer is option J. It is the only sentence that explains why the merchant went to the capital city. The other options supply information, but they are not relevant to the question.

Page 18
A possible answer could be: The writer of the editorial makes a strong case for cleaning up the river; on the other hand, some readers may not agree that the situation is as serious as the writer argues.

Page 19
Possible answers include using colorful language in describing the river during different seasons of the year; anticipating and answering opposing viewpoints; using highly charged words like *garbage, cesspool, shockingly,* and *disgrace*; and appealing to emotions by asking readers to restore the river for the benefits of their children and grandchildren.

Page 20
The correct answer is option G. The writer feels that now is the time to start cleaning up the river; others, however, may think another time is better. Each of the other options are facts that can be proven.

Page 22
A correct answer should include these points: The moonlight at night helps communicate the speaker's thoughtfulness and homesickness; the mention of frost gives a chilly and lonely feel to the speaker's thoughts; the mention of the mountain makes readers feel that the speaker is cut off from his own familiar surroundings.

Page 23
It is written in the first person because the speaker is one of two people taking part in the action described. A clue is the word *we* in the third line; it means "you and I," so you can tell that the speaker is acting in the poem. The word *our* in the last line also tells you that the speaker is a character in the events.

Page 24
This information should be given on the lines following "Previous Volunteer Experience." It could also go in the section "Special Skills."

Page 25
Option H is the answer. You can find this information by looking in the second column from the right, under the heading "Length (miles)." The six longest rivers in the world are all over 3,000 miles long.

Page 26
The best place for this step is between "Send out announcements" and "Assemble participant list."

Page 27
Here's a sample answer: Walk south to the corner of Plum and Vine, then turn right on Vine. Go to the intersection of Vine and Main and turn right, walk north on Main, over the bridge, to 1st Street. Turn left and walk past Pine Ave.

Page 28
Yes, it probably does, on pages 40–50. Chapter 3, "Into the Heart of Africa," sounds like it's about great African rivers like the Congo and Niger.

Page 29
Here's a possible answer: The Latin word *aestus* means "tide or surge," and the estuary is where the river surges into the ocean and the ocean tide meets the river.

Language

Page 41
The correct answer is option F. *My*, the first word, *Luigi's Ristorante* (a proper noun), and *Italian* (a proper adjective) are all capitalized. The sentence is a statement that ends with a period. Option G should end with a period. In option H, *Mom* should not be capitalized because it is not used in place of the mother's name, and *italian* should be capitalized. In option J, *Mom* and *Town* should not be capitalized.

Page 42
The answer is option J; it is the only sentence that uses a hyphen incorrectly. *One-third* is used as a noun, so it should not have a hyphen. In option F, *ready-to-eat* is a single adjective. In option G, *twenty-nine* is a compound number. In option H, *three-fourths* is a fraction used as an adverb, which modifies the adjective *finished*.

Page 43
Option F is correct. The words *the wing-nut assembly* are extra material inserted in the original quotation. In option G, there should be parentheses, not brackets, because the words *Is he crazy or what?* are apart from the meaning of the sentence. Brackets are used only when the sentence is a quotation from another writer. In option H, the parentheses should enclose *Shawn prefers the first one*, not *which movie*. In option J, the phrase *on her next birthday* should not be in parentheses because it is a necessary part of the sentence, not apart from the main meaning.

Page 44
Option H is the answer. The second independent clause is preceded by the conjunction, *and*, so there should be a comma between the two clauses, not a semicolon. In option F the interruption, *David*, is correctly set off by commas. In option G, the two independent clauses are correctly separated with a comma followed by the conjunction, *but*. In option J, the dependent clause that begins the sentence is correctly set off from the rest of the sentence by a comma.

Page 45
The answer is option F. The word *thinking* is not a past or present participle; it is the present progressive tense of the verb *think*. In option G, *ordered* is a past participle that modifies *camera*. In option H, *fastened* is a past participle that modifies *boat*. In option J, *thinking* is a present participle that modifies *Melanie*.

Page 46
Option F is correct. The underlined gerund phrase is used as the direct object. It answers the question, What do I enjoy? In option G, *standing on the corner* is a present participle phrase modifying *man*. In option H, *stopping* is part of the gerund phase used as the subject, so it should also be underlined. In option J, the underlined part is a pronoun, *what*, and the past progressive tense of the verb *think*.

Page 47
The correct answer is option H. *Her* agrees in number (singular) and gender (feminine, since Tiffany is female) with *Tiffany*, the antecedent of the pronoun and the indirect object of the sentence. Option F is neuter, not feminine. Option G is the form of the singular, feminine pronoun used as a subject, not as an object. Option J is plural.

Page 48
You should have chosen a word that describes the feat of climbing a high mountain. Possible adjectives include *difficult, challenging, fearsome, dangerous,* or *frightening*.

Page 49
The answer is option H. This one is tricky. Even though it begins with the word *where*, it makes a statement, rather than asks a question. Therefore, it is a declarative sentence that should end with a period. The other three options are interrogative sentences that correctly end with question marks.

Page 50
You could have written something like this: Like young lambs in a pasture, the fluffy white clouds scampered across the blue sky. This rewritten sentence begins with an adverb phrase and eliminates the unnecessary repetition of the word *sky*.

Page 51
Option J does not use correct parallel construction. For the sentence to be parallel, it should read: Bratwursts can be fried, broiled, or grilled on a barbecue. All the other options use correct parallel construction; similar sentence parts use the same grammatical constructions.

Page 52
Option G is correct. The appositive, *the world's second-longest river*, helps identify and give more information about the Amazon. Option F uses coordination to link two equally important ideas. Option H subordinates the less important information, *whom you've never met*. Option J subordinates the less important information, *which is a challenging game*.

Page 53
The answer is option H. It follows the rule for one-syllable words: double the consonant before adding an inflection like *-ing*

Page 54
Option H is misspelled. The correct spelling is *temperature*. Pronouncing the word correctly with four syllables might have helped you notice that the letter *a* was left out.

Mathematics
Page 56
The correct answer is option F. Comparing digits from the left, you find that the 3 in 13 is greater than the 2 in 12. In option B, the second 1 in 11 is less than the 2 in 12. The fraction 1/2 in option C is less than 1, so it is also less than 12. Option D is a negative number, so it is also less than 12, a positive number.

Page 57
The correct answer is option G. Multiplying 4.5 times 0.1 eight times gives an answer of 0.000000045. This is the base number preceded by seven zeroes.

Page 58
The correct answer is option G. The procedure for subtraction is the same as for addition. First convert the first number to a base times 10^4 by moving the decimal in the base one place to the right. This gives a problem of $91.0 \times 10^4 - 3.6 \times 10^4 = 87.4 \times 10^4$. Then, convert the answer to a whole number and a decimal, which leaves a correct final answer of 8.74×10^5.

Page 59
The correct answer is option H. The LCD for 8 and 3 is 24. Multiply the numerator and denominator of 7/8 times 3 and the numerator and denominator of 1/3 times 8 to get fractions with like denominators of 24 (21/24 and 8/24). Then subtract the numerators to get 13/24.

Page 60
Option F is the answer. The product of 24 and 35 is 840. The product of two numbers with different signs is a negative number.

Page 61
The correct answer is option H. Moving the decimal point in both dividend and the divisor makes the problem 19,202 ÷ 529 = 36.2986, rounded up to 36.299.

Page 62
The correct answer is option G. Find a reasonable estimate by rounding 7414 to 7500 and 289.6 to 300. Remove the digits in the one and tens columns to get a simplified problem of 75/3. A reasonable estimate of the answer is 25. The actual answer is 25.6.

Page 63
The correct answer is option F. The numbers 9, 12, and 18 can all be divided evenly into 144. In options G and H, 14 cannot be evenly divided into 144. In option J, the LCD of 24 and 56 is 168.

Page 64
Option H is the correct answer. Divide each term by the GCF of 7. 63 ÷ 7 = 9. 49 ÷ 7 = 7, for a ratio of 9:7.

Page 65
The correct answer is option H. The formula for finding the volume of a triangular prism is $v = 1/2\ lwh$, or $v = 1/2\ (9 \times 6 \times 10) = 270$.

Page 66
The correct answer is option F. With this scale, the largest bedroom that would fit on the notebook paper is 16 feet x 20 feet, a large bedroom. An average size bedroom, 10 feet by 12 feet, would fit comfortably on your paper. Option G is way too large to fit on a paper; a drawing on this scale would be half the size of your bedroom! Option H is too small; the drawing of a typical size bedroom would be 1 inch x 1.2 inches! In option J, the largest bedroom that would fit on the paper is about 4 feet by 5 feet, the size of a closet.

Page 67
Option H is the correct answer. This is another rate problem with several steps. First, compute the amount of interest Calvin will earn over the year by multiplying $750 x 3%. This total, $22.50, represents the amount of interest that will be added to the money he originally invested; this $750 is called his principal. The sum of the principal and interest paid is $772.50, the amount he will have in his account at the end of the year.

Page 68
The correct answer is option G. Did you see that the figure created by points B, C, and D is a right triangle? Because it is, you use the formula $a^2 + b^2 = c^2$ to find the length of line BC, which is actually the hypotenuse of the right triangle formed by points B, C, and D. If side BD is a and side CD is b, the answer looks like this: $9^2 + 12^2 = c^2$ or $81 + 144 = c^2$ or 225. The square root of 225 is 15, which is the length of side b.

Page 69
Option F is correct. Because angle C is an obtuse angle, you must find the other obtuse angle in the second figure that matches, which is angle X.

Page 70
The correct answer is option F. It has been flipped along line JI. Option G has been slid down and to the left. Option H has been slid down.

Page 71
The correct answer is option G. Replace both x variables with the value 4 to get (3 x 4) − (4 + 2) = 12 − 6 = 6.

Page 72
Option G is correct. Plug the values into the equation to get (6 x 3) ÷ 2 = 3 x 3 = 18 ÷ 2 = 9. None of the other options will result in an answer of 9.

Page 73
The correct answer is option H. Each of the points marked on the line solves the equation correctly. Option F shows the graph of the equation $x ÷ 3 = y$. Option G shows the graph of the equation $2x = y$.

Page 74
The correct answer is option G. The range is the difference between the greatest and least value in the data set. Subtract the lowest temperature, 4, from the highest, 25, to get 21. Option F is the greatest value. Option H is the mean. Option J is the median.

Page 75
The correct answer is option J. Even though you are throwing the dice at the same time, the principle is the same as if you were throwing them one after the other. You still need to figure the probability of the two events happening. In order to get a 12, you need to throw two 6s; this is the only combination that makes 12. Therefore, figure the probability that you will get a 6 on one die (1/6) and the probability that you will get a 6 on the other die, too (also 1/6). Multiply them together to get an answer of a probability of 1/36 of throwing 12.

Page 76
The correct answer is option H. You need to find a combination that adds up to 14 votes, half of the 28 total votes. With 5 votes for soccer, 6 for football, and 3 for tennis, their total is 14. The other options all add up to a different total.

Page 77
The correct answer is option J. This problem has three steps. First, figure the total cost of their food by adding the price of each item: $25.00. Then multiply this total by 0.15 (15%), the amount they want to tip the waiter: $3.75. Finally, add the tip to the cost of the food to find their total cost: $28.75.

Page 78
The correct answer is option H. Rewrite the proportion as n/6 = 25/30. Using cross products, 30 x n = 6 x 25 = 150, or 30n = 150. Divide each side by 30 to isolate the variable on one side. This leaves n = 5. The missing number in the proportion is 5: 5/6 = 25/30.

Practice Test: Reading

1. A
2. G
3. You could have written something like this: The Mississippi River takes on a different character during its journey to the Gulf of Mexico, from gentle and clear, to rushing and sediment-filled to broad and majestic. The paragraph is a discussion of how the Mississippi changes character and appearance over its length.
4. F
5. Probably the most important point your answer could have made is this: For both, the Mississippi is vital for transporting people and cargo.
6. G
7. C
8. The most important similarity is that both were explorers trying to claim the Mississippi for their own countries; the most important difference is that DeSoto was Spanish and La Salle was French.
9. B
10. J
11. A
12. You could have written something like this: The Mississippi River had a powerful effect on the people who knew it, including a young boy in Hannibal, Missouri. He grew up to be the great writer Mark Twain, who helped immortalize the river
13. C
14. F
15. D
16. J
17. You could have written something like this: An old woman from Kentucky traveling to New Orleans on a riverboat is frightened of boat racing. However, when a race begins, her love of racing overcomes her fear. She contributes her cargo of lard to the ship so that its boilers can burn hot enough to win the race. It includes the main points of the story as well as the conclusion.
18. H
19. B
20. Words with a negative connotation you could have written are *ancient, timeworn, fogeyish, worn-out, antiquated,* or *on her last legs*. Words with a positive connotation you could have written are *aging, elderly, aged, mature, mellow, advanced in age,* or *along in years*.
21. C
22. F
23. You could have written a description like this: The story takes place on a grand Mississippi riverboat traveling on the river toward New Orleans.
24. F
25. D
26. J
27. C
28. Here's a possible answer. Minneapolis will probably be significantly larger because it is growing, while St. Louis is losing population quickly
29. B
30. G

Practice Test: Language

31. D
32. F
33. B
34. You should have chosen a word that describes how the geese rose into the sky. Possible adverbs include *slowly, majestically, quickly, suddenly,* or *abruptly*
35. C
36. G
37. A
38. J
39. C
40. J
41. B
42. G
43. C
44. F
45. B
46. J
47. A
48. J
49. C
50. G
51. C
52. G
53. You could have written something like this: Many people may be surprised to learn that salamanders are not related to reptiles such as lizards, snakes, and crocodiles. One major problem with the paragraph is that all the sentences begin with the subject, followed by a verb. The rewritten sentence is longer and contains a dependent clause for variety.
54. You could have written something like this: Amphibians begin life under water, breathing with gills; as they age, however, they develop lungs and become land creatures. This rewritten sentence is a compound sentence that eliminates the repetition of the word *they*.
55. A
56. H
57. B
58. J
59. D
60. Adverbs modify verbs, adjectives, or other adverbs. You should have written a sentence with a word like *badly, well, really, slowly, majestically, quickly, fast, suddenly,* or *abruptly* in which the adverb is used correctly to modify another word.

Practice Test: Math

61. D
62. G
63. A
64. H
65. D
66. G
67. B
68. F
69. D
70. H
71. C
72. G
73. A
74. H
75. B
76. J
77. C
78. G
79. C
80. H
81. B
82. F
83. C
84. G
85. D
86. G
87. A
88. G
89. C
90. J
91. A
92. H
93. B
94. J
95. C
96. F
97. C
98. G
99. D
100. F
101. B